Wrestling With God

WRESTLING WITH GOD

Religious Life in Search of Its Soul

Barbara Fiand

A Crossroad Herder Book

The Crossroad Publishing Company

New York

1996

The Crossroad Publishing Company
370 Lexington Avenue, New York, NY 10017

Permission is gratefully acknowledged to excerpt from the following:

From *Leadership and the New Science*, by Margaret J. Wheatley. Reprinted with permission of Berrett-Koehler Publishers, San Francisco, 1994. All rights reserved.

From *Theology for Skeptics*, by Dorothee Soelle, translated by Joyce L. Irwin, Augsburg Fortress, 1995.

From *Will and Spirit*, by Gerald G. May. Reprinted with permission of HarperCollins Publishers, New York, 1983.

Printed in the United States of America

Library of Congress Cataloging-in-Publication Data

Fiand, Barbara.
      Wrestling with God: religious life in search of its soul / by
Barbara Fiand.
         p. cm.
        Includes bibliographical references.
        ISBN 0-8245-1620-6 (pbk.)
        1. Spiritual life—Christianity.   I. Title
BV4501.2.F43   1996
255—dc20   96-22811
                            CIP

*To Clare, Kay, Pat, Fran, Mary Kay,
Joyce, Kristen, and Sally,
and to all women and men religious
who are wrestling with God,
that, with the dawn,
we might receive a blessing,
and that God might grant us
a new name.*

Table of Contents

Preface

"Religious life today is like an egg ready to hatch, with new life eager to burst forth. The problem is that we keep taping up the cracks in the shell whenever they break open, because we want to preserve the 'integrity' of the egg." These remarks, made by a friend of mine during one of our many conversations around this topic, illustrate well the concerns of this book. Over the last several years, I have asked myself often why, with all the talents, gifts, intelligence, and potential that we collectively embody, so little is really happening to restore viability to our life. How is it that so many highly educated, highly motivated women and men seem so incapable of effecting truly significant change in their way of life and their corporate potential? What is happening to us and why? When I think of the thousands of religious throughout the world who yearly sign up for workshops, seminars, retreats, and institutes to reflect on and learn about the call to transformation, I know that we care, and that we are interested in our future, our communities, and the mission. Why is it, then, that religious life as we know it is dying, and what can we do about it? This little book is my contribution to this inquiry.

For those who will read it in quest of an answer, a clear explanation, a solution to our dilemma, however, this book will most likely be a disappointment. "There is a fixed time for everything under the sun," Scripture tells us. Ours does not seem to be the time for answers but, much more clearly, the time for questions. There is something sacred about questions; about looking into the issue, facing the crisis, releasing oneself into the pain, and embracing the mystery. It takes courage to abide in darkness, to wrestle until dawn. The struggle is always intensely personal. No one can do it for another, yet each of us, through perseverance, can help the others. Ours is the time for courage.

Questions, when asked rightly, lead deeper and open up possibilities. Questions can be healing, sustaining, empowering. Too often we shy away from them. We are afraid of the vulnerability to which we are exposed when we do not seem to have the answer or know where we are going. Questions teach us, however, that there is strength in vulnerability, and wisdom in not proclaiming the answer if its time has not yet come. Part I of this book invites us into vulnerability; into the asking of questions and the surrendering of our expertise. Part I of this book is a prayer for wisdom.

Part II is a prayer for freedom and a call to love. For too long religious have been struggling to do this, divided against themselves. The time has come to embrace wholeness, to come home to ourselves, to celebrate the vow that sanctifies incarnation, to inquire into its past and reflect on the meaningfulness of celibacy today. Nothing is more freeing than the acceptance of one's embodiment and of the creative energy that flows there. An honest discussion concerning affect and the holiness of intimacy is long overdue among religious. I hope this section of the book will help to foster personal reflection and to create a safe environment for sharing.

Part III is a prayer for openness to the new, for inclusivity. It is a challenge to honesty, a plea that we "walk the talk." Our foremothers and forefathers have left us with the distinguished heritage of going where no one else would, of loving and caring where no one else would. They were pioneers in the truest sense of the word, innovators in Christ's name. We carry their spirit with solemn responsibility. Today, perhaps more than any other time in history, the new is beckoning. Many are going in search of it for their own gain. But our task is to embrace the new creatively for the Gospel.

In a previous book, *Where Two or Three Are Gathered*, I wrote at length about the need for "participatory consciousness," about the relational level of awareness that is calling us from our comfort level in functionality and bureaucracy toward radical transformation. Part III of this book attempts to concretize the relational in our lived reality, to help us face it honestly and probe its implications. To illustrate the global dimensions of relationality, this section offers a brief excursion into the monumental shifts in perception that are occurring through discoveries in science, presenting themselves to us for our self-understanding. Nothing today is as it used to be. To be creative, therefore, requires knowledge and appreciation of the past, as well as open-ended dialogue with the now. "The path is made in the walking."

Because no book is worth reading unless it invites participation, each part of this book offers reflection questions for purposes of dicussion and personal response. The chapters within each part are brief in order to facilitate focused reflection. Our times are critical. All of us are needed, and no one can afford to withhold her or his wisdom from the group. It is my hope, therefore, that the questions will stimulate depth sharing and communal insight within our congregations, between congregations, and throughout the whole church.

I have attempted to write these pages in as inclusive a language style as possible. My hope is that this will provide the opportunity for both women and men readers to see themselves represented in, and to identify with, the events discussed in this book. Except for the rare occasions when the meaning of the text would have been distorted, any omitted generic female or male pronoun has, therefore, been added to citations, or else the plural form has been adopted. Because of this, a few citations may not be as smooth in the reading as might be hoped, and I apologize for this. In the interest of inclusivity, I ask the reader's indulgence.

Once again, I owe many thanks. This book was written during a very busy academic year and took a great amount of my time away from those who could have legitimately claimed it. I am most grateful to my sisters and friends for their patience and encouragement. There are many who have helped me in the writing as well. Among the thousands of women and men throughout the world who came to workshops, institutes, and study days, many will never know of how much value their questions, observations, and challenges were. I write this book for them. My special thanks, as always, go to Clare Gebhardt, S.N.D. Her critical reading of the text was invaluable to me, but even more so her vision, her guidance, her inspiration, and her wisdom. To Kay Brogle, R.S.M., my thanks as well, for interesting and useful imagery, for long conversations and heartfelt encouragement interspersed with healthy skepticism. To Pat Underhill, S.C., my thanks for being on the cutting edge and sharing probing questions and brilliant insights with me. My gratitude to Fran Repka, R.S.M., Joyce Lehman, C.P.P.S., Kristen Corcoran, O.S.F., Mary Kay Leuschke, P.H.J.C., and Sally Sherman, R.S.M., whose thoughts and ideas have been invaluable. To Sandy Lopez-Isnardi, a special thank-you for the cover art work so generously offered upon a simple request. I thank, once again, Crossroad Publishing for continued support and encouragement. I am grateful also to: Berrett-Koehler Publishers, Inc., for permission to quote from *Leadership and the New Science;* to Fortress Press for permission to quote from *Theology for Skeptics*; to Harper & Row Publishers for permission to quote from *Will and Spirit;* to the Religious Formation Conference and the National Religious Vocation Conference for permission to use material from articles previously written for and published by them; and, finally, to *Sisters Today* for publishing excerpts from Part I of this book in advance (January 1996), helping to "spread the good word."

I

On Asking the
Right Questions

A Myth and a Message

The legends have it that Arthur's knight, Parsifal, in his travels, comes, one evening, upon a lake where he sees a richly attired man fishing from a boat. The man gives him directions to a nearby castle, where he invites him to stay the night. When Parsifal arrives, he finds himself welcomed and honored by the same gentleman he had seen earlier and discovers him to be the king of the land. The Fisher King, as he is known, is a man deeply wounded since his youth and languishing in severe pain from which he can get relief only by fishing. He is extremely weak, cannot stand erect, and is incapable of performing any of his kingly duties. His realm is suffering greatly, and no one seems able to help.

That evening, Parsifal discovers that the Fisher King is the keeper of the Holy Grail. Every night there is a magnificent procession venerating the Holy Grail, which glows with a deep light from within and nourishes all who are present, granting even their unspoken wishes. All benefit from the Holy Grail except the Fisher King who, "tries to receive the nourishment and healing the Grail can give but, because of his wound ... is unable to take the healing."

Now, since Parsifal has found the Holy Grail, it is incumbent upon him to ask the great question: "Whom does the Grail serve?" This question would liberate the keeper of the Grail from his affliction and set his realm free. But because Parsifal is too preoccupied with, and amazed at, everything that is going on, he fails to ask this question. The meal ends, the Fisher King is carried out of the room, and all the guests depart. Parsifal also retires. In the morning when he awakes he finds the castle empty except for his saddled horse. As he rides out, the castle vanishes behind him. There is nothing left but the forest.[1]

A few months ago, in the early morning hours of a rare vacation day, this ancient Christian legend found its way into my waking moments and held me captive with unusual persistency. I had had a night of restless sleep during one of Cincinnati's record hot spells. Having just returned from the East Coast and a six-day guided retreat for some fifty women religious, many of whom had also come for individual direction, I found myself in a particularly vulnerable state. My experience had been grace-filled as well as painful. Walking with women religious at this time in our history, especially in the moments of personal reflection and prayer that a retreat provides, always seems to bring out my own vulnerability and need for self-reflection. It was not unusual, therefore, that the days following had been filled with thoughts around the experience I had just had, and that I found myself praying for the women I had walked with, sharing, in many instances, their pain and being with them in their struggles.

What came as a complete surprise to me, however, and found me totally unprepared, was the intensity of energy that surged through me that particular morning. I found myself waking up rapidly, and I sensed an urgency to reflect more deeply on the story that had emerged in me and to consider its particular relevance for religious life today. There was no doubt in my mind that the myth was directly related to the topics that had been part of the retreat, and that somehow I needed to work through its implications. Although dream interpretation and twilight imagery are not new to me, the timing of this experience, as well as its intensity, caught me completely by surprise. I had neither the free moments nor the desire to write, but somehow knew I had to.

The legend of the Fisher King is a fragment of the much larger Grail myth with which many of us are familiar, especially as it pertains to King Arthur and the knights of the Round Table. I had just recently read Robert A. Johnson's analysis of it in reference to the wounded male psyche of contemporary times[2] — a psyche whose feeling function has been wounded through socialization. That morning, however, this legend struck me as speaking directly to the issues facing religious life today and offering itself as a paradigm for our reflective self-analysis. Myths and legends, as is well known, lend themselves to various levels of meaning and provide a broad spectrum of interpretation. It is, therefore, not unusual or strange that one can see a story that has been used to deepen understanding of the wounded male psyche as applicable to religious life generally. The connection, in fact, struck me as more real than we might like to think. Has not our entire lifestyle been interpreted for years now, and for some of us since our "formation" years, according to the rubrics of a very masculine canonical structure?

Salvation and healing, so the legend tells us, comes through the readiness and willingness on the part of life's traveler to ask the *right question.* Parsifal (the personification of humankind) encounters the deeply wounded Fisher King (our inner core and truest self) who, being "too ill to live but unable to die,"[3] as Robert Johnson words it, invites him into the Grail castle. Too preoccupied with the issues of the moment and his own identity concerns — rescuing fair maidens and fighting dragons — Parsifal, upon seeing the Grail, is unable to ask the redemptive question that would heal the Fisher King and liberate his realm. *That* the Grail is there fascinates him; *why* it is there and *whom it serves* are not yet concerns for him. The crucial direction that this question would have opened for him, therefore, is denied him, and he leaves the next day to concern himself once more with the "circumference" of life, having missed its center[4] and the Holy One who dwells there.

Fortunately, later on in the myth we are assured that, in due time, life allows Parsifal a second chance. It often does so for us also. This usually happens during those graced moments when, through suffering and the general disenchantment that accompanies every call to conversion, we are faced with the opportunity for reexamining our values and for looking at the deeper questions of our existence. Parsifal, therefore, gets another invitation to return to the Grail castle and to question into the *why.* "Whom does the Grail serve?" opens him to the insight that "the meaning of life ... lies in the service of that which is greater than one's self. ... [T]he meaning of life is to relocate [one's] own center of gravity,"[5] to surrender to the depth within that has been wounded by one's own denial and "crucifixion"[6] of it, and thus to find healing and wholeness.

The Danger of Denial

A lengthy analysis of this story in terms of Jung's theory of the Self as the archetype of God and of each person's deepest center as wounded, goes beyond the scope of this reflection.[7] My concern, as I have mentioned already, is rather with this legend's symbolic significance for us as religious at this point in our history and in our culture. The confusion — even alienation — and the sadness many of us experience today is, I believe, matched in intensity only by our denial of it, especially in the public forum. "It is very dangerous," says Robert Johnson, "when a wound is so common in a culture" — and, I would add, in a family, a specific group of people, an institution, or a congregation — "that hardly anyone knows that there is a problem."[8] Johnson observes that in Western civilization there seems to be "general discontent with ... life but almost no one knows specifically where to look for its origin."[9] Kierkegaard called this condition "sickness unto death," and my sense is that congregationally it is touching almost every facet of our togetherness, even as we refuse to question into its meaning and blithely proclaim "new beginnings"; draw up long-range plans; write corporate objectives; and strategize about affiliates, associates, and intercongregational novitiates as if we were bursting at the seams and burgeoning all over with energy and enthusiasm.

Just recently a letter discussing the planning phases for the General Chapter of one large and aging congregation came to my attention. The consideration of death and decline during these days of common reflection and discernment was clearly stated as a "non-option." This congregation has four pre-vowed members in the United States, and a median age in its various U.S. provinces of between 59 and 74. There is an eerie unreality in this kind of attitude — an attitude that is dangerous because it is blind, sinful because it shuts out the resurrection.

The legend describes the Fisher King as "being too ill to live, but unable to die." The condition that keeps him this way, as I mentioned already, is an inability (perhaps in our age it is an unwillingness, a fear) to ask the right question. And so the Fisher King — *that inner self in all self-aware organisms (be they individual or corporate) that supplies them with energy and life; with meaning, and motive, and vision* — languishes. Oh, the processions are held regularly, and the Grail in its splendor is venerated — the symbols and traditions remain, the proper decorum is preserved, the rituals are lovely— but the soul languishes. And that soul is *our soul:* We talk charism and insist on how unique our presence in the Church is; how important it is to "form" people in our traditions. We come together and organize our insights on newsprint, which we then summarize and type out — maybe even proclaim in calligraphy on our walls. We speak piously and hold on to what we know "should" be said. We talk of more prayer for vocations, form recruiting teams of energetic and happy religious, have occasional dinners for interested persons, advertise through the media, and get involved with the Internet, but our soul languishes. And because we do not notice, as in fact Parsifal did not, the Grail (which serves the Holy within) slowly disappears again. And we "ride out" from our assemblies, our committee meetings, our study sessions, even our Chapters, to busy ourselves once more with the issues at hand: to get ready, no doubt, for more meetings and further studies, with more newsprint and summaries. But the soul languishes, and the energy depletes. Because we are unable or unwilling and afraid to die, the resurrection escapes us.

A religious from a large and, by reputation, quite forward-moving congregation wrote to me a few months ago in response to a questionnaire I had drawn up in order to assess the relevance of congregational documents and meetings in the lives of religious generally. This is what she said:

> I have participated in three of our General Chapters. ... Each of them in their own way left me feeling a kind of sadness, each time for different reasons. With some I felt that we refused to look at the implications of our actions, with others I felt that we did not speak out of the lived experience but wrote of ourselves in glowing terms. Sometimes I felt that we were writing for others and not for ourselves. We constantly were trying to use everyone's pet word or phrase and putting together a statement that finally really said nothing because it tried to say everything. Most delegates seemed to leave Chapter with such high hopes and I tried to go back to my group and speak with some fidelity to what the Chapter had done, but always with a nagging feeling. To speak in less than glowing terms of what was done was always greeted with the charges of being negative.[10]

The prophetic, of course, has almost always been interpreted as "negative." It is often uncomfortable and risks the possibility that someone "might get hurt." It alone, however, opens the door to "creative dying," calls us to authenticity and courage, and challenges us on behalf of truth toward new possibilities.

Elsewhere I have reflected on the Easter question: "Why do you seek the living among the dead?"[11] and have suggested that one of the major difficulties for us at this time in religious life is the fact that not all of us are equally aware of what is dying, let alone of what is already dead in our midst, and so we keep holding on to it and even venerate it. We cannot recognize the death that *needs* dying before the resurrection can happen. Some of our structures and traditions may be too ill for meaningful existence today. We are, however, unable to let them go because we dare not question their relevance. Interestingly enough, an alternate version of the Parsifal legend has him refrain from asking the liberating question, not because he is not curious or even aware of its importance, but because chivalry forbade inquisitiveness, and he had been taught never to intrude by asking questions. The relevance of his behavior to religious decorum needs no further reflection. In what recently I have heard referred to as "dysfunctional civility," we also, too frequently, shy away from the difficult issues because we do not want to offend anyone. The questions not asked, the problems not addressed, the traditions not challenged thus become a noose around our neck, stifling the energy we need for creative action and courageous change.

Not long ago one of my friends reflected sadly on her experience of religious life: "There's a great deal of life among us wanting to be born, and we're going to kill it, because we are refusing to go into labor." Her remark brought home to me the amazing relation between dying and birthing. It occurred to me that in the physical order both processes ultimately enter a stage of inevitability, where choice is nil and surrender mandatory. Though many a mother, during labor, may have wondered what on earth she had done to herself in becoming pregnant, there is no way out except through; and in the agony, new life emerges. Death too, our faith tells us, is like that. Nature is simple here and quite compelling. The difference between our natural processes and their numerous spiritual, social, and psychological parallels throughout our life, lies in freedom. Whether a mother surrenders or not, her baby *will* be born. Whether or not, as dying persons, we accept our death, it ultimately *will* overtake us. The dyings of customs, of ways of thinking, of modes of behavior, of world views, of systems and traditions, however, depend on willing surrender, on *human freedom*. In these instances, too, there will be no resurrection without death, no birth without labor. But our freedom can easily choke new life, and the lethal presence of that which refuses to accept death (the ghosts of our past) can stifle and even poison creativity for centuries. Babies who cannot be born die, and so do the mothers who cannot give passage. Mothers cannot choose such catastrophes, but *we* can. Systems and unchallenged traditions can deny passage. In their blindness they eventually, of course, choke themselves as well, but the catastrophe is in *their* choosing. How aware are we of this danger? Are we willing to go into labor and birth the new, or will we choke the fledgling life in our midst because we do not want to let go? In seeking the "living among the dead," are we honoring tradition, or are we not in fact belittling it?

On Tying Up the Cat

Perhaps a simple story in a lighter vein can help to illustrate our dilemma: *Once upon a time there lived a guru in an ashram who every night when he sat down to pray found himself disturbed by the ashram cat. He decided that, in order to allow himself as well as his brothers to pray in peace, he would have the cat tied up during prayer time. His idea worked well. Now, a few years later the guru died. The monks were in consternation as to what to do with the cat, and upon lengthy debate (always, of course, aiming at consensus), it was decided that they would continue to tie up the animal during prayer because, after all, the guru had ordered it. Then one day the cat died. Once again the monks were puzzled as to what needed to be done. They decided, finally, to purchase another cat so that it could be tied up during prayer, just as it had always been done ever since the time of the guru.*[12] It would, of course, not be surprising if all sorts of theories arose thereafter about the liturgical significance of tying up cats during evening prayer.

Tradition is not respected when we hold on to it meaninglessly. Then, like tying up the cat, it becomes ridiculous. And continuing to do things solely so that no one will be offended only trivializes the once-creative idea and de-energizes those held captive by it. Then, our decisions around the undeniable problems facing religious life today (an aging and depleting membership, the relevance of our lifestyle, a lack of clarity around the vows and around the manner in which we welcome new members, to mention but a few) are a mere rehashing of old formulas. We choose denial of that which defies understanding or of that which is too painful to face, by engaging in an endless listing of "if only's": "If only we would do this, go back to that, demand more of this." Our "if only's," however, do not dwell in the *now*, and it is the *now* that claims us.

In my lighter moments I describe tradition simply as "a good idea that worked." Because the person who had the idea was particularly holy or venerable, however, it became enshrined under the rubrics of TRADITION. And, sadly, in many cases no one has been allowed to have a good idea since. It is, of course, true that we need to distinguish between Tradition and traditions, so that we will not lose the former as our sacred trust while we critique the latter. I am not at all sure, however, that many of us in this age of crisis can even agree on *what* distinguishes one from the other. Many mere customs or outdated canonical regulations have indeed reached the status of the "venerable" among us precisely because we have found it inappropriate — out of place — to examine the inner dynamics of our life together and to ask the difficult question: "Whom do they serve?"

Robert Frost's poem "Mending Wall" comes to mind: There the poet questions the meaningless mending of a stone fence that serves no purpose at all, since it holds nothing in and nothing out anymore — the pastures having been replaced by pines and orchards. Each spring, however, his neighbor faithfully engages in the ritual of mending the wall that nature is wearing down, because his father, and most likely his grandfather before him, had seen it as a value. Watching him, the poet reflects:

> Before I built a wall I'd ask to know
> What I was walling in or walling out,
> ... Something there is that doesn't love a wall,
> That wants it down ...
> ... I see him there
> Bringing a stone grasped firmly by the top
> In each hand, like an old-stone savage armed.
> He moves in darkness as it seems to me,
> Not of woods only and the shade of trees.
> *He will not go behind his father's saying,*
> *And he likes having thought of it so well*
> *He says again, "Good fences make good*
>   *neighbors."*[13]

It seems to me that we, too, in many respects, "move in darkness," and refuse to go behind our fathers' or mothers' sayings. We hold on to what we have always done and see value in behaviors and actions that have long outlived their meaning. We are even proud of our faithfulness as we continue to mend the fences that separate us from the "real" world we are called to serve.

In this regard, perhaps, the ministry of welcoming new members into our midst (traditionally referred to as "formation") is the most blatant case in point. I will return to this topic more extensively later. Suffice it to say, here, that the expressed (and, sadly, also the often unexpressed) difficulties and frustrations, as well as the high stress level experienced by the vast majority of newer members speak for themselves. Our need for, but persistent lack of self-criticism regarding our entrance policies (in spite of the plethora of meetings we hold around this topic) is evident not only in the poor response to our vocation efforts and in the frequent departures of newer members, but also in the erratic behavior and unhappy attitude exhibited by many of them toward the whole process of discernment and evaluation *we* plan *for* them. "Grin and bear it," their professed friends advise, or "If you really want this life, jump through the hoops. Once you make final profession, things will change." What is it that leaves our traditionalism here so clearly unaddressed, and turns our well-intentioned welcome into an imposition of rules and regulations, requiring freedom and maturity to be checked and left at the novitiate door? Whom do we serve if we keep "tying up the cat?"

Because Parsifal was unable to ask the right question, the possibility for depth was withdrawn. All that remained for him was an empty castle and an obsession with his identity as a knight doing knightly deeds, while his inner core lay languishing without creativity. I fear that religious identity and all the regulations we insist on to maintain it; our constant rewriting of mission statements; our numerous questionnaires and self-studies; our endless debate on entrance procedures and "formation" formulae; and even our Chapter acts, valuable though they may be, run the danger also of pointing to an empty and ultimately a vanishing castle, while our soul, our inner core, our founding inspiration, languishes.

Joan Chittister, in an article written in the *National Catholic Reporter* (February 1994), speaks powerfully to the *now* that claims us: "The only question for this time is, will religious life go on in us or will others have to come to revive it? Two things are sure: First, groups who do not deal with the questions of the day cannot possibly leaven the time. Second, where passion is lacking, life is dead."[14] That religious life will continue in one form or another does not seem to be the question for Chittister and others who have studied the history of this phenomenon through the centuries. Contrary to what is often suggested, religious life has undergone numerous variations and transformations throughout the ages and, in the Christian tradition itself, has had many diverse expressions. As Philip Sheldrake puts it: "[R]eligious life is not so much a single spiritual tradition as a variety of movements and Christian life-styles which, because they interrelate, are generally viewed as a single phenomenon."[15] We need not worry, therefore, that its survival will depend on *our* survival. Others will undoubtedly come to revive it in ways most likely quite different from ours — avoiding perhaps those pitfalls that caused our demise. In a certain sense, I suppose, that can be quite reassuring, but what a tragedy it would be, nevertheless!

On Healing Our Passions

The symbol of the Fisher King languishing, so Robert Johnson asserts, points, in our day, to the neglected feeling function.[16] It is wounded in an age that ridicules tenderness and worships toughness; that hails reason and has little use for affect. Our culture values clear objectives, certainty, clarity, and closure. It fears the heart. It dreads ambiguity. It shies away from risk; from living into the questions that arise in times of transition and crisis, when old paradigms are collapsing and the new is only now emerging and calling us to patience and vigilance. I do not believe that as religious we can afford to dupe ourselves by the notion that we are counter-cultural in this respect. We too have neglected affect, and only *we* can heal our passions. Elizabeth Johnson says it well when she remarks that religious life "has become domesticated by too close an identification with the law, structure, and spirituality of the institutional church." With Diarmuid O'Murchu, she contends

> that religious life in the West needs to reclaim its limi-
> nal identity, a move of genuine conversion entailing *pro-*

17

found change in spirit and structure. Religious would
then be known as persons and communities who *are in
touch* with the sacred, passionately committed to justice and *loving relationships.* ... They would stand in
church and society as liminal, archetypal, prophetic persons, *articulating and empowering the deepest love.*[17]

But for this to be possible, we need to accept our wounds
and address the difficult issues. In this regard Robert Johnson
warns us that "probably the worst pain ever experienced is the
self-inflicted suffering that has no cure outside one's self."[18] Its
anguish is exceeded perhaps only by the endless and meaningless suffering that comes with denial and gnaws away at the
very marrow of life precisely because it is not acknowledged
and dealt with.

"Where passion is lacking, life is dead," writes Joan
Chittister, and she gets specific: "When religious life is routine,
the life is dead. When religious life is bent on being socially
safe and legally proper, the life is dead. When religious life is
more an ember than a fire, the life is dead."[19] Our blindness to
these symptoms results in the marginalizing or even the rejecting of our "own weary prophets," and in the resistance many of
us exhibit to the questions that would make us effective in, and
relevant for, our time.

The "marginalizing of our prophets" is, of course, never as
overt as the expression would have it appear. We simply ignore
them when they offer their services. Sometimes, to assuage our
consciences, or to "show our good intentions," we tell them how
gifted they are, and how much the congregation needs them.
We invite them to dinner to ask their advice, which we promptly

ignore or file away under the heading of "idealism" or "radical views." And if the community should discern their leadership potential and call them to service, those who ultimately hold power neutralize them by giving them harmless tasks to do, so that the status quo can be maintained, and none of our traditions are threatened. Thus their spirits are shackled until, in order to survive, they seek to express their creativity elswhere. The congregation, in turn, rids itself of the questions they might ask and the issues they might call us to address.

In this regard the observation that Ladislas Orsy shared with a colleague of mine many years ago strikes me as rather noteworthy: First-class leaders, he suggested, surround themselves with a first-class team and support staff. They are not threatened by the gifted and do not hesitate to let them express their talents and call forth the future. Second-rate leaders, on the other hand, will avail themselves of second- and even third-rate advisers, for they need to see themselves as superior and cannot afford to have their role-tied identity threatened. Sadly, with second-rate leadership the prophets move beyond the institution that stifles them. They become marginalized, our "weary prophets," as Chittister calls them, and in their absence religious life dies.

Today it is imperative, not only for our survival, but much more importantly for our relevance and for the Gospel that we profess, that we reject simply holding on to the status quo for its own sake, no matter how comfortable it makes us feel. Today, more than ever before, corporate entrenchment needs to yield to a passionate committment to systemic change that not only has us call all creative visionaries to the fullness of their potential, but also has us work in full and open cooperation with every other like-minded and like-hearted institution. Religious isolationism — the separation of the sacred and the profane, of religious and laity, and even of diverse religious congregations (always in the name of our charism, of course) — is disastrous for the mission. Congregational protectionism has no place in a universe called to radical transformation. Today we are called to a relationality heretofore unheard of; to cosmic consciousness that has no room for pettiness and self-centeredness. If our vision fails us here, our life is dead. And so, Chittister continues: "Then, religious may pray and they may fast and they may withdraw from the fray, but they will not sound a single note in a cacophonous world in search of harmony."[20]

A Time for
Courageous Waiting

I am reminded here of a remark made to me by a woman religious who works with a great many congregations in the various capacities of a facilitator, but now has taken a resolve to refuse contracting with any group "that is simply re-arranging the deck chairs on the Titanic." When a ship is sinking, considerations about neatness or aesthetics are useless, but so are organizing prayer meetings, fasting, and withdrawing from the fray. When a ship is sinking, bold and unshakable courage is required, a courage neither frantic nor rash, but rather honest and strong; a courage that can let go of non-essentials in critical self-awareness and stand in empty humility and in waiting. "The real truth about religious life right now is that ours may not be the time of resolution," Chittister concludes, affirming my introductory observations. "Ours may be simply the strong, faith-filled, exuberant era of questions that is given for living into a new generation of answers. Ours may be the waiting time."[21] It is interesting that Heidegger sees waiting in the most profound sense as *serving*. By waiting reverently and with keen sensitivity to the exigencies of our time, we serve the truth as it unfolds in our midst.

Several years ago, I presented this understanding of waiting as fundamentally connected to the vow, as well as the virtue of obedience; as, indeed, basic to our Christian call to depth listening.[22] Perhaps today, more than ever before, our maturity, both individually and corporately, depends on it.

> We live ... in a broken world and, in our radical union with this world, are ourselves broken. Our Christian mission, if it is to be healing both for ourselves and others, must come to grips with its own wounds. The questions which present themselves cannot be answered glibly but must be "lived into" with passionate endurance and waiting. As Heidegger reminds us in his *Letter on Humanism:* to wait means to listen, to be vulnerable, to be poor as a shepherd is poor. Living "into" the question is experiencing the answer in its depth dimension: as a deeper question which does not own the truth as "clear and distinct," but shepherds the mystery.
>
> All this may sound discouraging. We are, after all, children of the age of technology — the age where science promises to leave no problems unsolved, no questions unanswered. ... It is difficult, therefore, to stand in the pain of a question without demanding a resolution. It is difficult, even more so, to face the issues of our time and wait in humility for the proper questions wherewith to address them. Here is, however, where I see fundamental obedience as the unifying force whereby the evangelical counsels can be affirmed, truly lived today, and whereby holistic — mature — community can happen.[23]

Our struggle with all this is enhanced, I believe, because any measurable result is rather difficult to attain when one deals with matters of personal, as well as congregational and even cultural, maturation.

The bureaucratic mindset, furthermore, that marks our mode of interacting even to this day[24] is clearly hard pressed to fathom what could possibly be meant by the "proper questions," especially if they do not demand an immediate and clearly stated resolution. We are so used to the drawing up of questionnaires and to the professional analyses of these questionnaires; to getting things finalized and feverishly holding on to deadlines and corporate progress reports, that *abiding in the waiting, patient listening, living into the question,* simply does not make sense. My suggestion in *Where Two or Three Are Gathered* that General Chapters give themselves to this task rather than to Chapter acts, and that they invite the entire congregation into the questing,[25] is an attempt to move us in that direction. The question is: Do we dare? Many of us seem to prefer rearranging deck chairs as our ships are sinking, for we cannot comprehend what possible good anything else would do.

Lao Tsu's question comes to mind here:

Who can wait quietly until the mud settles?
Who can remain still until the moment of action?[26]

His reflection, later on, would serve us well:

A truly good [person] does nothing,
Yet leaves nothing undone.

> A foolish [person] *is always doing,*
> Yet much remains to be done.[27]

Lao Tsu's "creative waiting" has nothing at all to do with mindless abandon to the vicissitudes of life. One hopes that all of us would question such passivity and pessimism. It has everything to do, rather, with an acute awareness of the present world situation, with organizing research and "think tanks" around matters of global concern, with inviting experimentation and visioning, with fearlessly situating our traditional behaviors and values into the here-and-now and examining them contextually. It has everything to do with open eyes and with the trust-filled loving that *caringly* walks this culture asking the liberating questions.

Leadership in this regard is urgently needed among us. General Chapters, especially, must recognize, once and for all, that the time for creating numerous documents, for nitpicking about and arguing over wording, for the endless calling for more and more intercongregational meetings, for wordy proclamations and the multiplication of corporate reports is over; that the time for inviting depth reflection and interiority is now at hand and is, in fact, long overdue. Our corporate status is hardly in question, nor is it challenged by anyone, although we seem to exhibit an almost chronic obsession about clarifying our stance and defining ourselves. We have, in fact, become rather good at definitions, at identifying our objectives, at actuarial studies, and at the general management of our affairs. Many of us handle large amounts of money and administer huge institutions that we can be proud of. But, in the process, *the healing and liberating question of our collective myth* seems to be taken for granted —

as if we were really always holding it, as well as its answer, before our eyes; as if the "service of the Grail" really concerned us, and all our corporate decisions were clearly expressions of our founding inspiration and our baptismal obligations.

We have indeed become very busy and, some of us, even very important. Can we, however, truly be still enough for ultimate concerns? Can we let the question, in all its starkness, challenge us and change our lives — not just individually, but collectively? Can we be together any length of time and, in the words of Lao Tsu, "attending fully ... *be without cleverness*"? "[B]eing open to all things," are we able to "do nothing"?[28] Rahner's exhortation keeps haunting me: "Face loneliness, fear, imminent death! Allow such ultimate, basic human experiences to come first. *Don't go talking about them, making up theories about them, but simply endure these basic experiences.* Then in fact something like a primitive awareness of God can emerge."[29] Whereas, without this humble openness to depth, "Religious life is and remains really of a secondary character and its conceptual thematic expression is false."[30]

The Need for "Core" Involvement

Now, when we finally give ourselves over to them, the questions that will open up and invite pondering may, indeed, disturb many of us. It will soon become clear to us that no one body of persons, no matter how well qualified and gifted, will be able to handle them alone, for they will demand radical shifts in vision and, therefore, require congregation-wide interest and creativity. The questions for today will *need* all of us. They will, therefore, challenge our common notions of leadership. They will call each of us, perhaps more than ever before, to personal commitment and resolve. The questions for today will move us beyond administrative categorizations. They will defy percentiles and render most statistics irrelevant, if not meaningless. They will not be satisfied with a momentary "filling in of blanks" on handouts sent from the motherhouse, for they will involve us *to the core*.

More than anything else, the questions for today will need to reflect our connectedness with the *now* and our awareness of the gifts, as well as the wounds, of today. Depth is not achieved by hankering after the past, no matter how good it was, but only by creatively integrating it with the present. Today, knowledge of science and technology, of psychology and developmental issues, of theology and holistic spirituality is essential for every religious. Today, only personal responsibility for, and an interdisciplinary approach to, who we have become and where we want to go will allow us to ask the right questions and effect our healing.

That such a challenge will call for a profound revisioning of obedience is beyond doubt. The emphasis on personal accountability, on vision that involves all of us and calls each of us to ever deeper questing, clearly points to an understanding of obedience that stresses autonomy (from the Latin *autos* meaning self, and *nomos,* law) and values maturity, personal decision making, and responsibility. It is important to recognize that our choices are, of course, always made within a covenantal relationship. This protects mature obedience from isolationism and individualism. It does not, however, absolve anyone from the deliberative process.

The capacity to work within a non-curatorial model of community (where everyone is expected to think and discern, and where normal decisions are made by normal adults who neither need parental guidance or approval nor have to worry that every minutia requires group discernment) is, of course, not acquired merely through intellectual conversion. The "tapes" of our training years in religious life, and even in Catholic education, are not easily erased and are heavily laden with guilt. The military "command performance" cycle of religious obedience, furthermore, is deeply rooted in the patriarchal tradition that has enveloped us from the cradle. Its *a priori* status of holiness has rarely, if ever, been questioned. It was, after all, tied to Jesus' obedience unto death,[31] to Abraham's instant will-ingness to kill his son and offer him as sacrifice. Canonized as such, it was our working model, and the questionable theology supporting it is only now being reflected on.

There are, therefore, many among us who will shy away from any revisioning of this vow. They will, no doubt, continue to declare that heteronomous (from the Latin *heteros* meaning outside, and *nomos*, law) obedience to the dictates of those "wiser" or even "holier" than their flock fostered sanctity among religious in days gone by and brought about many great works for the reign of God. In the light of contemporary scholarship, however, the speciousness of such a view, especially when it is used as an argument for maintaining the status quo, can no longer be ignored. It seems particularly dangerous when nostalgically held forth for congregational refounding. Historical research today lays open the suffering and cruelty endured by many of our founding communities, and the unwholesome, unjust con-ditions in which they were forced to live. The developmentally regressive regulations enforced upon many communities in the name of holiness can no longer be dismissed as ultimately salu-tary. Nor should they ever be extolled as exemplary, even if enacted by founder or foundress, no matter how well intentioned he or she may have been. Studies dealing with our founding and with past theologies of religious life, furthermore, cannot be excused any longer for ignoring ecclesial dualism and its almost universal oppression and infantalization of women. These theologies need to be radically revisited and contextualized. Their relevance for today needs to be questioned. They need to be rethought, and present traditions based on them that continue to foster unnecessary dependency on the one hand, and autocracy on the other, need to be named as such and then abandoned.

What I am suggesting here is that reverence for the theological traditions of our Church alone is simply not enough any more. These traditions, too, had their interdisciplinary roots, and must be understood and criticized within their historical situation. Past behaviors and values are not, ipso facto, holy. They were often based on erroneous assumptions derived from the philosophies and sciences of the time that are no longer applicable today. Some examples here may help to clarify. Much of the Church's view regarding sexuality clearly pertains to what we are discussing. It influenced, in fact often seriously hindered, a healthy understanding of celibacy for most of our predecessors. Even to this day, it resists a much-needed reexamination. For a holistic understanding and embracing of this vow; its roots in Stoic self-abnegation and rejection of affect; and its affinity with Augustinian dualism, hatred of pleasure, and of all things feminine, need to be clearly identified and let go of. The mediaeval caste system associated with the denial of sexual love and its corresponding chances of eternal glory[32] remained with us, in one way or another, well into this century. It is incomprehensible to most of today's adults, and its motivational power with regard to celibacy is nil. An honest rethinking and regrounding of our vow, based on contemporary scholarship, is, therefore, absolutely necessary. This is so not only for religious who wish to live it in a wholesome and healthy way, but also for Christianity generally, since it holds our way of life as clearly one way of living out the baptismal call toward holiness. Nor should we delude ourselves, in this age of liberal thought, that adequate work in this regard has already taken place.

Healthy and open dialogue dealing with human sexuality still seems extremely rare in most congregations. My own attempts at evoking thoughtful conversation related to celibacy among the religious in my seminars is almost universally acknowledged by them as a first, though a sorely needed, experience. We will return to this topic in a later chapter.

A second, and perhaps more general, example illustrating the desperate need for contextualizing tradition can be found in the seemingly unchallenged reverence for and canonization of "permanence in the midst of change" that influenced every facet of ecclesial life, from the proclamations of dogma to perpetual vows and sacramental character. What was holy was unquestionably forever — an indelible and indubitable affair — universally defined and cast in eternal rules. The origin of this view is, once again, clearly rooted in the world view, cosmology, physics, and even politics of antiquity.[33]

Today we know that reality is not static and is, in fact, much more correctly understood as organic; change, therefore, and with it growth, viability, and health are concepts as well as values applicable to the cosmos. Today we know that we are part of the cosmic organism and, as conscious life, are responsible for it in an intimate love relation. We know, therefore, that matter and spirit are no longer juxtaposed but deeply interconnected. We know, from the discoveries in holography, that each part of reality actually contains the whole;[34] that nothing is insignificant any longer, that the Vine is in the branches and the branches are in the Vine. We know that union with one another and work toward personal as well as collective healing has cosmic implications. We know that competition and power fixations, even for the holiest of motives, spring from illusions concerning the nature of reality and ignore the interconnectedness of things. And although the metaphysics of the past explains the reason for, and helps us to understand, a fixed world order, today its thought system simply no longer has any credibility, and the static theology suited to antiquity and to many of the unquestioned values it engendered is rapidly losing its meaning.

On Regrounding Our Values

This does not mean, as Nietzsche's Madman wanted us to believe, that all values will need to be abandoned and have, in fact, been rendered useless.[35] What it *does* mean (and here is the reason for the creative waiting and mature obedience we have been discussing) is that those values need to be rethought and regrounded. Some may, indeed, lose their eminence; others may rise in stature. What is required above all, however, is radical honesty — the ability, the willingness, and the courage to question into the why of things without fear of rejection or worry about giving scandal.

"Why are we celibates today? What is the point?" are questions, for example, that do not automatically imply a negative attitude or signify the desire to do away with what has been valued for so long and by so many diverse traditions. What they *do* imply is that the reasons for the stoic celibacy that influenced the early Fathers[36] may no longer be satisfactory, nor hold motivational power for the religious of today. What they *do* imply is that celibacy, an evangelical counsel, as it was promoted by the early Fathers and throughout the Middle Ages, needs revisiting, and that the value of this way of life needs to be grounded in reality as we know it today.

Similarly, what does it mean to be poor for us who seemingly are not? Can we claim this vow for ourselves in any respect without becoming laughable in this time of massive destitution? Does "solidarity with the oppressed" perhaps better describe what we mean? And are we truly in solidarity with them? If holography is right, is the whole of this world — including its brokenness — contained within our hearts? Are our hearts breaking? Can we change our systems so that their hearts too might break in solidarity with the oppressed? A friend of mine observed the other day that most religious congregations today seem to worry primarily about money and about aging, yet many of our founders were poor and aging when they started. Nevertheless, they did great things because they were led by broken hearts that contained the world. What has happened to us since our founding?

These questions neither affirm nor deny the old interpretations, but show the need, rather, for examination and contextualization. It does not seem possible today to be destitute as well as effective in the elimination of this economic abomination. No one should "cultivate" poverty. Nor ought we look for opportunities to "feel" what poverty is — to learn lessons in it, if you will, by visiting the inner city with the intention of "getting it firsthand." Too often, I fear, T. S. Eliot's lament, "We had the experience but missed the meaning,"[37] applies to our good intentions, as we organize "experiences" for everyone, including our "novices." Solidarity needs to be deeper than that. It needs to speak to the poverty within and to the blessed encounter with our own deep-down helplessness, powerlessness, and even sinfulness. Paul's cry of destitution in 2 Corinthians 12:7-9 had something to do with poverty, I believe, and Eliot's reflection belongs to him: His

> "... approach to the meaning restores the experience
> In a different form, *beyond any meaning*."[38]

Paul, thus, surrenders to the words: "'My grace is enough for you, for in weakness power reaches perfection.' And so I willingly boast of my weakness instead, that the power of Christ may rest upon me." Paul is poor.

Still another set of questions seems pressing enough to mention here: What of the value of membership? Why does full membership in most religious congregations require perpetual vows? Is permanence necessarily better? Is anything ever final? Would religious congregations benefit, perhaps, from restructuring their membership requirements? Why are we seemingly so frightened of moving beyond known structures? Is it cruel, perhaps, to suggest that there might be a deep-down elitism that gnaws away at our life and diminishes us in spite of our protestations of inclusivity? Within that context, who are our associates, our lay volunteers? Do they really feel they belong, that they are one with us? Or have we, in fact, merely established a "branch office" for our charism with them — under our control and direction, of course, lest they become too visible? Do we treasure their presence? How *do* they join us? Do we long to *join them*, or do we merely need their often large numbers so that we do not have to be confronted quite as starkly by our own diminishment?

I am reminded here of an experience that one of my own

sisters shared with me several years back when she had been commissioned to explore the possibility of establishing a lay volunteer program for our congregation. She was very enthusiastic about this project and traveled around the country interviewing directors, as well as members of such programs. During one of her interviews with a lay director of a large and thriving program, the director asked her why her congregation was interested in forming such a program: "Do you want us to join you so that you can 'empower' us"? he asked. "If so, don't bother, because we are already empowered. Do you want us to join you so that you can teach us how to pray? If so, don't bother, for we already pray. Do you want us to join you so that we can work together for the reign of God? If so, do invite us in; we are ready and eager." Where do we stand with questions like these? What are our motives? How do we really see ourselves in a Church that is clearly and steadily, even though at times reluctantly, moving into the age of the laity?

Although the questions we have been considering can easily be judged as originating in unseemly liberalism or simply in a fickle attitude, might they not, instead, express an honest recognition of the present reality? Might they not, indeed, arise out of a deep appreciation (perhaps for some as yet unconscious and, therefore, difficult to articulate) for the flow of energy in the universe, for developmental matters, for the dynamics of human relationship, for the change that comes to all of us with personal maturation? In the case of poverty, might they not arise out of a recognition among religious concerning the urgent need for the experience of personal fiscal responsibility that is concomitant with all realistic adult living today? Could questions such as these perhaps be born from deeper values and a changing theological perspective hitherto unrecognized or unknown? Might they perhaps originate from a wider sense of community, from an appreciation of Church and charism that longs to embrace in action, not just in words, the entire human family; reach out beyond gender, ethnicity, status, and sexual orientation for friendship, and fellowship, and sharing? And, as mundane as this may sound, could it be that they may even flow from our contemporary training and wisdom regarding systems analysis, adult learning, and group motivation, or from general organizational expertise?

Whatever their origin, we can no longer avoid the fact that questions such as these are now being asked around the globe. Sometimes they are discussed quietly in support groups of two or three; sometimes, congregationally, at meetings where they are often "tisked" away into silence. Sometimes they are merely whispered in the anguish of our individual hearts. They are questions of intense struggle. They often arise out of deep pain. They are questions that involve dying as well as new hope. We ignore them only at our own peril.

On Wrestling with the Angel

A brilliant and stirring essay by Dorothee Soelle, recently translated into English and entitled "The Unknown God," situates
these questions for us where, I believe, they belong: Soelle
meditates on Genesis 32:22–31 — Jacob's encounter with
God, his wrestling with the angel. She writes of an *assault* on
Jacob and of a *blessing,* and asks: "Who is God in this story?"
She is not interested in and does not inquire into the meaning of
Jacob, for she already *is* Jacob. She is well acquainted with
having "to cross over a river" — with rites of passage and "being expelled from childhood"; with the anguish and anxiety of
the human condition. "I seek out the other one, the one who
assaults," she writes. "I seek the one who blesses. ... I am not
interested in Jacob but rather in his goal, his abyss." She wants
to know the meaning of Jacob's cry to God: *"I will not let you
go,"* and claims: "I do not want to *cite* this sentence, I want to
act on it."[39]

It seems to me that the questions we are asking today concerning religious life and its relevance for the gospel are in this
deepest sense, somehow, a wrestling with God. They are wrench-

ing questions that not only deserve but, in fact, mandate the struggle. They are questions for all of us:

> Each one of us wrestles with God
> let us stand by that
> even if we are defeated
> and put out of joint
> each of us wrestles with God
> who waits to be used
> A struggle waits for us.[40]

We cannot let God go until God blesses us. But the blessing is *in the struggle,* and *the prevailing,* and thus *in seeing the face of God.*

> Each of us is blessed
> Let us believe in that
> even if we want to give up
> Give us the brazenness to demand more
> Make us hunger after you
> teach us to pray: I will not leave you
> that simply cannot be everything
> A blessing awaits us.[41]

The struggle of religious life lies in our goal, our abyss. As we strive for authenticity in what seems so clearly to be falling apart, we can either surrender to the banal, to the inconsequential, and drift gently into oblivion, or we can, as Jacob did, persevere through the night and courageously face the contemporary encounter with God: Face the questions of our time and involve ourselves passionately in a world that needs transformation.

The choice, clearly, is ours, and by it we will live or we will perish. We can continue to worry about policies and procedures, entrance requirements and evaluations, mission statements and filling in forms, budgets and average expenditures per household, statistics and median age. Thus we can assure ourselves that, when our congregations fold for lack of life, everything will be neatly organized. We can, however, also put our emphasis elsewhere. We can listen to the depth within and to God's Spirit groaning there for the liberation and the conversion of our lives. We can surrender to the truth to which we belong, as we tend to broken hearts in a broken society. We can take the risk of getting messed up as we involve ourselves in a messy world from which we are no longer "set apart" — a world that we passionately love and to which we finally know we belong. We can let ourselves admit that struggle is of the essence in the experience of conversion; that the God of our time assaults us in our pious complacency and will not let us rest; that encountering God today means enduring the night. Our "gods have fled," Heidegger maintains, and the encounter with God requires suffering through the greatest darkness.[42]

There is no doubt that, at present, night prevails. The struggle with Jacob took place then, and he did not know whom he was fighting. The *assault* of God today is in the meaninglessness of our time; in the violence, the indifference, the horror of war in the name of a "new world order"; in rape, and incest, and child abuse; in AIDS and starvation right here in the land of "the brave and the free," and across all of civilization. The *prevailing* is in the involvement, in the care, in the primary concern, in the passion for justice, in getting our hands dirty. The *blessing* is in the soft heart and the knowledge of relevance even if no new member ever darkens our door again, and no synod ever concerns itself with us again, and no constitutions ever get approved again. The blessing is in the sisterhood and brotherhood of God's family to which we belong, not as "chosen few" but as *one-with.*

> Praying and struggling belong together. Who is the God of Jacob and our God? Who assaults Jacob, and who blesses him? Who comes to us as fate, as disastrous drought, as material constraint, as the stranger, the unknown one who afflicts us? The answer does not lie in theology but rather in the wrestling that we may call prayer or struggle; they amount to the same thing. God assaults us no less than God assaults Jacob. In prayer we present ourselves to the one who assaults us. We are naked; we have sent away that which could protect us. Let yourselves be assaulted by God; do not think that Jabbock lies far away. ... Everything speaks in favor of struggling with God for God, that God may become visible, that God's sun may rise in us also and we may receive a new name.[43]

Unfortunately we, too often, tend to mistake strife for mere over-againstness and see prevailing as "winning over." Thus, we miss the profound relationality of struggle. "I will not let you go," says Jacob to God, "unless you bless me." In response, he receives a new name, signifying at once power and destiny. The God of our struggle, of our abyss, is the God of our destiny also. Its blessing is ours in the prevailing.

The God Who Appears
at Dawn

Not long ago during a faculty in-service lecture I heard this God of our destiny referred to as the "one who lights fires and hammers rocks into pieces" — no doubt a reference to Jeremiah 23:29. I found this reference particularly interesting since the lecture seemed strangely supportive of the academic structures that so many of us find counterproductive and of the institutions that house them. What *are* the rocks, I mused (as my mind shifted back to religious life), that need to be hammered into pieces if our congregations will, indeed, *prevail* and be *blessed*? Our speaker referred to "institutional intractables." I thought of the entrenchments and unmovables of a fixed world order that has provided the underpinning for much of our spirituality. That world order mandates conservative stewardship and the clear mechanisms of control that are still heralded so frequently by the institutional Church, and that, in spite of declarations to the contrary, many of us seem to treasure also. I asked myself whether religious institutions as we know them today are really *able* to work for God's reign and to "light God's fire" in truly *new* ways? And, then I thought of Eckhart praying that "God rid him of God," and wondered whether perhaps this is what *we* need to pray for? Perhaps our image of God brings about entrenchment. Perhaps our spirituality needs to be "hammered into pieces." I know that in many instances our religious vocabulary has changed, but have our insights, really; has our vision?

A strange story of the kind of "hammering" I am referring to is passed on to us in Persian mystical poetry. There it is told that Moses one day heard a shepherd praying to God in the simple and homely way of shepherds: He spoke of wanting to help God — of fixing God's shoes and combing God's hair, of washing God's clothes and picking off all lice. He wanted to bring God milk and kiss God's hands and feet before he went to bed. He wanted to sweep God's room and keep it neat and tidy. He told God that all he could say when he thought of God was "Ah!"

It is said that Moses became quite irritated with the shepherd's apparent disrespect. He told the shepherd that the one who made the earth and sky should not be addressed that way; that God does not need shoes and socks and milk; that this kind of talk was blasphemous and sounded more like a conversation with one's uncle. Only something that grows needs milk; only someone with feet needs shoes and socks. Moses suggested that the shepherd's love was foolish and irreverent and advised him to use appropriate language.

The story tells us that the shepherd repented when he heard Moses' admonition; that he tore his clothes in sorrow, sighed and wandered into the desert. Moses, on the other hand, had a sudden revelation from God, who reprimanded him for separating God from one of God's own. "Did you come as a prophet to unite or sever?" God asked. God pointed out that God has given each being a unique way of seeing, and knowing, and speaking wisdom. What often seems wrong to Moses may be quite right for the shepherd. Purity and impurity, sloth and diligence in worship, Moses was told, mean nothing to God, who is apart from all that. Ways of worship are not to be ranked as better or worse. It is all praise. It is all right. Contrary to Moses' view, it is not God who is glorified in acts of worship; it is the worshiper. "I do not hear the words they say," God instructed him, "I look inside at the humility. That broken, open lowliness is the reality, not the language. Forget phraseology. *I want burning, burning!*" God asked Moses to be friends with his burning, to burn up his thinking and his forms of expression. He suggested that those who pay attention to manners of speaking are of one sort. *Lovers who burn are another.*[44]

The God who "lights fires and hammers rocks into pieces," loves those who burn. Is our God a God of fire or a stickler for precedence? Do *we* burn? Do we worship, as the Russian philosopher Nicolas Berdyaev would have us, a God who is dynamic and passionate, a God who fits the universe God created, a God who knows tragedy and experiences it, a God who knows suffering and pain and is with us in ours? Berdyaev believes such a God, though truly Christian, is still far away from the Western psyche. Such a God still needs our struggle:

People are afraid to ascribe movement to God, because movement indicates the lack of something, or the need for something which is not there. But it may equally well be said that immobility is an imperfection, for it implies a lack of the dynamic quality of life. Tragic conflict in the life of the Deity is a sign of the perfection, and not of the imperfection, of the divine life. The Christian revelation shows us God in the aspect of sacrificial love, but sacrificial love, far from suggesting self-sufficiency, implies the need for passing into its "other." It is impossible to deny that the Christian God is first and foremost, the God of sacrificial love. ... Dramatic movement and tragedy are born of the fullness, and not of the poverty of life. To deny tragedy in the Divine life is only possible at the cost of denying Christ. ... This is the theology of abstract monotheism. Abstract monarchic monotheism which refuses to recognize the inner dramatism of the Divine life is a clear instance of the confusion between negative and positive theology. Creation of the world cannot be deduced from the Absolute which is perfectly self-sufficient.[45]

Berdyaev maintains that creation is held in the creative love energy of God. The creature is "a Mystery of love and freedom."[46] In us divine passion and human passion embrace; God's suffering and ours merge.

The question at issue for religious today is: Does Berdyaev's God hold sway in our hearts? Does Berdyaev's God fit into our lives and into our corporate and individual ministries — not just into our prayer circles and morning meditations, but into the decisions we make and the values we strive for, both individually and as congregations?

I am reminded, once again, of Joan Chittister's article and her plea that values of uniformity (often disguised in the language of corporate identity) and our top-heavy systems give way to releasing "everywhere in society, at every level, through every individual member, wherever those members are, whatever separate things they do, the white heat of the congregation's charism in one great corporate mind and one easily seen communal heart."[47] *Our God wants burning*! I ask myself: Is such releasing possible for us? I know it needs to be, and I long for it with all my heart. But will our present spirituality support this? Will our image of God support this, or will it first have to be hammered into pieces so that our hearts can burn?

For those of us training ministers and teaching theology, it has become abundantly clear that the image of God in contemporary times is changing radically. The "theology of abstract monotheism," of the unmoved mover, the uncaused cause; the theology of a God who makes and knows all the rules, of God the great manager of the universe and controller of destinies, has lost its credibility. In a post–Auschwitz, post–My Lai, post–Romero world, this kind of theology is meaningless. For the contemporary person struggling with theology's traditional responses to a world of almost universal doubt, an all-powerful God has only one relevant mandate: To end mindless and unjust suffering. And if God chooses not to, for whatever "logical" reason our theology can offer, this God becomes unbearable. "An all-powerful God who imposes suffering [or even is indifferent to it], who looks down on Auschwitz [on My Lai, on the death of Romero, on Sarajevo] from above, must be a sadist," writes Soelle. "Such a God stands then on the side of the victors; and is, in the words of a black theologian from the U.S., 'a white racist'. ... And a theology which conceives such a supreme governor, organizer, responsible cause and creator reflects the sadism of those who come up with it."[48] Authentic believers today can no longer experience God that way, nor do they want to. Evil as an "absence of Being," or as "ultimately salvific, in the greater scheme of things," falls into the category of the absurd, the obscene. Only a God who can suffer *with* us, a God who meets us in darkness and despair; only a God who "stands on the side of victims"[49] and turns our hearts of stone into hearts of flesh, is credible today and has any motivational power.

A viable theology of ministry embraces such a God. *Our ministries, whatever they are, and our very lives — the way we relate to and care for one another and our sisters and brothers beyond the congregation — must witness to such a God.* Soelle speaks of the woman who told her about her struggle with the Jewish-Christian problem. She said that when she finally had come to "understand Auschwitz" *she joined the peace movement.*[50] It is today no longer sufficient to explain the world's evil with neat ethical categories, nor is it enough to pray for the forgiveness of sins or the conversion of sinners. God *intervenes through us.* Our God wants burning.

The God who appears at dawn looks at us through the eyes of suffering people everywhere. A viable God in an age of ethnic cleansing and global starvation is neither self-sufficient nor changeless; is not beyond need or vulnerability. A God who is believable today does not "permit" suffering. A God who is believable today suffers with those who suffer. God weeps for them and does so *through us.* The ruler and hierarch, the king of kings and lord of lords, of course, does not. "Unmovable," he cannot, and so it is paramount that we pray God to rid us of him.

When we speak of God's pain, we employ another concept of God than the purely masculine one. God is then our mother [more inclusively we might see God as either parent], who cries over what we do to one another and what we do to our brothers and sisters, the animals, and plants. God comforts us as a mother [a dad] does: she [he] cannot charm away our pain (although that also happens occasionally), but she [he] holds us in her [his] lap long enough for us to stand up again and have new energy. God could not comfort us if she [he] were not bound to us in pain, if she [he] did not have this strange and wonderful ability to feel the pain of another on her [his] own body. To suffer with, to be present for another [*sic*]. The gospels describe Jesus as one who has this ability. If someone hits us on the face in his presence, he flinches, and feels it on his cheek. If someone is told a lie in his presence, his need for truth is present. If a whole person is suppressed under the brutal power of the empire, he weeps over his city, Jerusalem.[51]

In Jesus, the God of our abyss becomes, fundamentally, the Persian shepherd's God. In Jesus, God needs shoes, and socks, and milk. In Jesus, witnessed to and radically appropriated in our age by all *those who burn*, the image of God is rescued from the idolatry of kyriarchs[52] and becomes credible again. In Jesus, our God clearly is a suffering God, and we meet this God everywhere:

There [is] in him [her] no stately bearing to make us look at him [her],
nor appearance that would attract us to him [her].
He [she] [is] spurned and avoided by all,

a man [woman] of suffering, accustomed to infirmity,
One of those from whom [we] hide [our] faces,
spurned, and we [hold] him [her] in no esteem.

(Isaiah 53: 2,3)

God in Christ meets us today "among the godless, among the corpses,"[53] as the victim of torture and of ethnic cleansing; as the disappeared and the not-looked-for; as the refugee, the migrant, the homeless; as the hungry, the beggar, the outcast; as the lonely, the unpopular, the unattractive. God in Christ meets us in nature, ravaged by pollution and global warming; in animals, killed and tortured for human amusement or gain; in plants, destroyed by pesticides.

I received a letter not long ago from a Sister of Mercy in Auckland, Aotearoa-New Zealand, who is actively involved in establishing a creative and hospitable environment in her congregation so that new life can flourish. She signed her letter "A Star Thrower from Down Under." She had been at an Australian conference where I had shared with a large group of religious Marie Chin's version of Loren Eisely's now-famous story of the man he met at sunrise as he walked the beach near a seaside town called Costabel. Each morning, Eiseley

found people combing the sand for starfish which had washed ashore during the night, to kill them for commercial purposes. It was, for Eisely, a sign, however small, of all the ways the world says no to life. But one morning he got up unusually early, and discovered someone on the beach. This man was also gathering starfish, but each time he found one alive, he would pick it up and throw it, as far as he could, out beyond the breaking surf, back to the nurturing ocean from which it came. As days went by, Eisely found this man doing his mission of mercy each morning, seven days a week, no matter the weather. Eisely named this man "the star thrower," and, in a beautiful meditation, he reflects on how this man and his predawn work contradicted everything that he, Eisely, had been taught about evolution and the survival of the fittest. There on the beach in Costabel, the strong reached down to save, not crush, the weak. And Eisely wonders: Is there a star thrower at work in the universe, a God who contradicts death, a God whose nature (in the words of Thomas Merton) is "mercy within mercy within mercy" and who wants only life.[54]

God in Christ is this star thrower and longs for us to be star throwers as well in whatever we do — individually or corporately, in little acts or great deeds, for the congregation or for the larger community and, yes, even for ecology. God calls us to participate in, as well as to proclaim with our lives, "God's involvement in our human community and culture which is the place, the staging ground, for the crucially spiritual issues of power and love, of generosity and selfishness, of violence and compassion."[55]

This is why God in Christ *meets us also in our own darkness and wrestles with us there*. God asks us to face our anxiety, our brokenness, our despair, our personal as well as our congregational sinfulness and lack of integrity. Some of us God needs to lure from our "Babylonian captivity," by exposing us to our addictions, our compulsions, our fiscal anxieties and dependencies — the "illnesses of prosperity," as Soelle calls them,[56] which we so frequently, and often so ardently, deny. God also struggles with us in our poverty and our want; God perseveres with us in our "sickness unto death" until, hopefully, God can bless us and give us a new name.

The struggle for religious life today is the struggle for relevance, not only in the face of a questioning world "out there," but also in the depth of our own questioning hearts. The evil in our world challenges us to the quick. We wrestle with God at the very center of our being, both individually and congregationally. Our involvement in the suffering of this age can simply no longer remain peripheral to our "traditional" ministries. Nor ought it be relegated to a minority among us who work directly with the poor, or to our justice or social action committees, where the passionate few try in vain to get the rest of us involved beyond verbal commiseration. Our involvement has to take hold of us *at the core*. Our authenticity as Christians depends on it. Our integrity as religious will not survive without it.

It is said that the sin of Babel was not so much arrogance as it was the obsession with security. Wanting to rely on their own strength and capacity for self-protection and preservation, God's people forgot God in their midst. They became addicted to their need for security and their ability to buttress themselves against any intrusion. In so doing, they were alienated from within and could no longer "understand" one another. The reversal of Babel is Pentecost. Here the followers of Jesus got over their anxiety and trusted in the Spirit. The power of God, as fire in their midst, broke through the walls that gave them security and hid them from the world. Being healed from within, they cast off fear. They proclaimed God's word, and *everyone* understood them.

It is my sense that, as women and men religious, we desperately need to let ourselves be reclaimed by the Spirit of Pentecost. We need to have the rocks of our worries and insecurities hammered into pieces. We need to be reclaimed by the energy of the resurrected Christ. And then we need, with courage and trust, to take hold of the Gospel message that *death has lost its sting* and act accordingly. *Our God wants burning.*

Questions for Focus, Reflection, and Discussion

1. The Parsifal myth admonishes us to "ask the right question." It speaks of an inner core, too ill to live and yet unable to die. It calls us to move away from the circumference and into the center of life. How does this myth speak to religious life today? What is our wound? Are we in denial? Does our soul languish? Are we able to talk of our death, and if so, can we see this as a creative activity?

2. How is it with our congregational meetings? Do we shy away from the difficult issues with "dysfunctional civility"? Can we ask the liberating questions? What are they?

3. Tradition is not respected when we hold on to it meaninglessly. Then we in fact trivialize it. Can we distinguish between Tradition and tradition? What might the distinctions be? How does Robert Frost's poem apply to us?

4. How is it with the prophets in our midst? Do we marginalize them? Can we hear them, or do we prefer second rate leadership so that we can maintain the status quo?

5. What might it look like in our respective congregations if we were about "abiding in the waiting, patient listening, and living into the questions"? What might be the "healing and liberating question of our collective myth"?

6. In "The Need for Core Involvement" we are challenged to revision obedience. What does this mean, and what might this look like in each of our lives?

7. "Past behaviors and values are not, ipso facto, holy. They were often based on erroneous assumptions derived from the philosophies and sciences of the time that are no longer applicable today." What does this statement mean to you, and how do you relate to the examples offered?

8. How do you relate to the observations concerning poverty offered in "On Regrounding Our Values"? How about the questions offered regarding membership?

9. Is the religious life of contemporary times strong enough to wrestle with God? Are we empassioned enough not to let God go until God grants us a new name? What does this mean?

10. Does our spirituality need to be "hammered into pieces"? Do we need to pray God "to rid us of God"? What do these questions imply about our vision, our relevance in contemporary times?

11. Soelle tells us of a woman who, when she finally came to understand Auschwitz, joined the peace movement. What did she mean? How are religious today "star throwers"? Do we burn?

II

On Growing Into Freedom

In God's Image

In the westernmost part of Pennsylvania, the Sisters of the Humility of Mary have their motherhouse and a retreat center. On the grounds, not far away from the main building, one can find a little chapel that houses a statue of the Mother of God, brought over from France when the community first came to the United States. Mary is holding the Infant Jesus on her left arm. Her right hand and arm were broken off and lost, it seems, during the voyage overseas.

While I was making a retreat there several years ago, one of the sisters told me that, over the years, many an artist of the community has tried to restore the statue's hand and arm but always without success. Because of this, some of the sisters see themselves, in a special way, called to become Mary's right hand and arm. I remember clearly pondering the meaning of this during my retreat and for many months after. I remember also getting bolder during my days of prayer there and stretching my thought toward what it might mean to become the right hand of the *feminine side of God,* or of God *as Mother*.

It is true that such thoughts do not speak to all of us. The feminine side of God has, indeed, been neglected in our culture and, through some five thousand years of tradition, has perhaps not even so much as been recognized. As a consequence, woman as imago dei, and the archetypal feminine in men as well, are foreign concepts. Some may even see them as dangerous — as destroying "tradition," the "way we have always understood things," the "truth."

It is not my intention to discuss here the reasons for such one-sidedness and exclusion, nor to explain the theological relevance of the divine feminine. Others have done so already and eloquently.[1]

I merely wish to point to the impoverishment all of us — both women and men — have suffered because we could not and, sometimes, would not identify aspects of our personality, of our very being, as in "God's Image." I wish to suggest also that, if we have suffered theologically from this refusal, we have been deprived, even more so, psychologically, aesthetically, and emotionally. "One of the basic principles of classical aesthetics," we are told,

> says that only what proceeds from our gathered strengths can be called "beautiful." "Everything which is isolated is reprehensible," as Goethe says. Every separation of a single human potentiality, every overdevelopment of one strength at the cost of others is "isolation." The isolation of rationality requires that we suppress or deny our corporeality and our emotionality. Every expression of life, for example every human relationship as well as every creative activity, should be "whole" — that is, it should engage all our strengths. The more of myself that I forget, deny, repress and suppress in one

relationship, the more partial, the more limited, the more impoverished will be the relationship. One-dimensionality is the expression of such impoverishment and destruction. Although it can attain a specific perfection, it lacks the beauty which stems from the ensemble of our strengths, experiences, and relationships. A human being becomes beautiful in the experiences of the wholeness of his or her strengths, in uninhibited teamwork.[2]

The impoverishment due to the severance from, and neglect and depreciation of, the feminine in our culture is, I believe, experienced with particular acuteness in the affective areas of our lives. Religious are particularly vulnerable here. Due to the unmitigated rejection of our embodiment, spawned by an obsession with the evils of human sexuality that has plagued the Church from its earliest involvement with Greek culture, a healthy development of affect has been virtually nonexistent in our formative years. I am convinced that part of the struggle with God, considered in the previous section, lies, therefore, precisely in reclaiming the neglected feminine archetype, drawing from its strength, and letting its wisdom flow through our bodies — in declaring our severed parts as holy and allowing God to incarnate there.

Nor should we labor under the illusion that women are somehow exempt from this task by virtue of their gender. They too can be caught up in the denial. Being women does not automatically guarantee accepting and celebrating the feminine within. Too often, being liberated can be perceived simply as being admitted to pseudomasculinity in a woman's body, as being allowed to do what men have done heretofore, as operating in the "masculine" sphere, if you will, and adopting a "masculine way of perceiving reality without learning to appreciate the treasure hidden within [one's] own unique feminine way of being-in-the-world."[3] The feminine side of God needs appropriation by all of us. Its cultural belittlement, ridicule, and often universal denial has diminished all of us. Beauty "stems from the ensemble of our strengths," Soelle notes. One-sidedness is ugliness. It fosters blindness and underdevelopment. "If Christ is born a thousand times in Bethlehem," says Angelus Silesius, "And not in you/ You remain still eternally lost."[4] The Christification of *every part of us* is a baptismal obligation for both women and men. Holiness is wholeness and mandates acknowledging all — including the counter-sexual within. It means coming home to ourselves.

It is my sense that, for many religious, what I am discussing here is not new. Through the numerous committees, support groups, in-service days, and workshops that our congregations have organized for us in the last several years, we have at least been made aware of it. *But have we truly allowed ourselves to be changed, to be enriched?* Have we given ourselves permission to consider the culturally and ecclesially neglected and even despised aspects of our personality, to be reconciled to them, to see them *as part of God in us,* to celebrate them both personally and congregationally? Have we been freed? Have we been healed?

In the first part of this book, when reflecting on the Parsifal myth and its relevance to the wounded feeling function of religious life, I suggested that our entire lifestyle has been restricted and interpreted for decades, if not for centuries now, according to the rubrics of a very masculine canonical structure (Part I, "A

Myth and a Message"). As a consequence, it is not difficult to imagine that parts of ourselves have been split off, severed, atrophied, denied. The vibrancy of existence demands more than the confinements of law and structure permit. It needs passion and originality. It needs to acknowledge and embrace diversity and uniqueness, as well as the natural polarities of life. It needs to struggle with the flesh-and-blood issues of loving and relating that cannot afford denial. For us to become whole, therefore, as persons and as communities, we need to recognize our need for our unacknowledged and severed limbs. We need to nurture them back into life.

A Tale and a Message

Perhaps an ancient tale can help us, once again, to focus our considerations: *The story is told about a miller's daughter who finds herself the victim of her father's greed and subsequent dealings with the evil one. She successfully wards off being taken captive by Satan. The latter, however, does not leave her alone and orders her father to cut off her hands. After that, she flees from her father's house into exile. Eventually, she encounters a young king who lives in a beautiful garden. He falls in love with her, marries her, and fashions her a pair of silver hands. She bears a child and lives happily with the king until he has to go on a long journey. Once again the evil one interferes in her life. Satan intercepts and falsifies the letters between the couple. As a consequence, the young woman is banished from the realm, together with her child. She wanders aimlessly and experiences great desolation, loneliness, and suffering until she comes to a large forest. There, an angel of God meets her. The angel leads her into the depths of the forest, where she enters a house with the inscription: "All who enter here shall be free." She stays in the house for seven years while her natural hands grow back.*

When she can hold the world in her own embrace once more, her husband finds her. They are reunited and live in sacred union for the rest of their lives.[5]

We encounter in this story life's traveler once again: This time, a woman — deeply wounded and deprived of the capacity to touch, to hold, to feel, to be truly who she is. The silver hands, though fashioned with good intentions, do not restore her to wholeness. They do not heal. They simply enhance her external appearance and make her functionally acceptable in the world of her husband.

One might venture a guess that in the realm of interiority, of depth relating, of tenderness, of affection and all its incarnational manifestations, the symbol of the silver hands, that this story presents to us points to serious deficiency. Jungian analyst Marie-Louise von Franz sees in the woman with silver hands those elements of passivity and helplessness[6] that have afflicted women in our culture for millennia and are, in many cases, a cultural expectation of any "good" woman even to this day. Sometimes overtly, but more often in private now, many of us reject assertive and self-motivated women as unduly aggressive. We resent them in the male-dominated public office of government and Church and even resent the men who encourage them to use their gifts there.

Although it is mostly unacknowledged in our day and in our culture, there nevertheless seems to be only one norm whereby to judge appropriate behavior — the stereotypical masculine one. Judging by "silver-handed" standards, it holds court over all conduct — that of men and women alike — and fashions for us the means for appropriate interaction. In so doing, it negates those aspects of ourselves that do not comply, rendering them inactive and denying their potential for creativity. Being encrusted in a false one-sidedness — a dualism that separates the world into clear categories of spirit and matter, soul and body, good and evil, normal and abnormal, masculine and feminine, superior and inferior — the stereotypical masculine standard fosters the illusion of illegitimacy and abnormality in many areas of behavior. This, if it does not lead to denial, leads to self deprecation, to a sense of personal inferiority and self-hate, not to speak of the prejudice, gender bias, and discrimination it engenders.

Applied to religious life, it seems that the standard of "silver hands" has been honored with relative success for quite a while now, especially in the area of our ministries and in much of our congregational administration. The training we have received often blinds us to the artificiality of the structures that many of us still so ardently support. We have adopted them, committed ourselves to them, and find ourselves often quite at a loss even to envision a "better" or more equitable way of promoting God's reign. Some women religious (albeit an ever decreasing number) might actually see themselves as happily exempt from the implications of the story we are reflecting on, and of the cultural straitjacket it symbolizes. The professionalism to which we have dedicated ourselves with considerable success since Vatican II has, after all, given at least some of us access to numerous areas where our creativity seems to be appreciated. As far as men religious are concerned, the message of this story might even quite readily be perceived as a non-issue. It seems that they are imune to it, since, after all, they are recognized by everyone as the male servants *par excellence* of a masculine Church. The archetype of their primary orientation is being utilized, therefore, with full steam ahead.

My own response to this way of seeing things is, of course, rather skeptical. I wonder whether any of us is truly as free as some of us would like to believe. It seems to me that, as we journeyed through life, all of us have indeed had magnificent silver hands fashioned for us, and by well meaning people at that — our congregations, our families, and, more generally, our society at large that knows so well our place in the service of the Church. Ministerially, it is true, we are for the most part over-equipped both individually and congregationally. We function well there and are quite satisfied. For women's communities, if this were the criterion for supplying the feminine dimension of God to our Church, little would be missing. The point, however, is not that we are working well, but that *we are working well with "silver hands" fashioned for us by someone else.*

The question that demands our attention, therefore, goes deeper: How is it with our own personal lives? What about the depths of our own being — the soul, languishing within? How many of us can truly love ourselves as we love our neighbor and are energized by that love? How many of us have been enabled, and have enabled others, to do this through our covenant with one another? In our human interactions and relationships, have we been, and are we being allowed to grow our *own* hands and thus to become the hands of God?

We are, I believe, being invited by our times into a new frontier — a relational frontier. Paul admonishes us in Romans to love one another in our diversity (Romans 12: 4-13). Truly to love an other is to empower her or him to *be*: To be the expression of God here on earth out of an authentic realization of her or his freedom; to be fully grown, whole; to gain voice and to be released from fear; to be at ease and to embody a mature acceptance of herself or himself.

I am reminded here of an experience recounted by Christin Lore Weber in her book, *Woman Christ*. It happened during her early adulthood some 30 years ago. But somehow I feel it is still, at least symbolically, relevant for religious today:

> [J]ust after graduating from college, I taught speech and drama to a group of novices at a convent in the Midwest. The biggest challenge I experienced was *helping them find their voices*. Although these women were adults in their early twenties, their voices maintained the high, breathy quality of the small girl-child. No *power* there. These women had disembodied their voices and unempowered the expression of their thoughts. By so doing, they seemed to assume a submissive attitude every time they spoke, and the more they spoke the more submissive they seemed to become.
>
> All summer we exercised those voices, using tape recorders, body exercises, breathing exercises, yelling exercises — *finding the body's center, finding the voice's source*. At the summer's end, not only did the voices sound different — grounded, strong, assured — but the women themselves were different. They had begun to *locate a passegeway to their power.*[7]

Weber speaks of the denial of feminine power for which we ourselves are at least partially responsible either by silencing our voice or by denying our vision. In many ways, through nonresistance, we have cut ourselves off from the depth within, from the life-giving energy of the feminine. We have severed our own hands. The resulting impoverishment cripples us (both women and men) most profoundly in the relational sphere of our lives, in the feeling dimension of our being. To repeat Soelle's admonition: "The more of myself that I forget, deny, repress, and suppress in one relationship, the more partial, the more limited, the more impoverished will be the relationship."[8] Relational wholeness cannot happen without the primary, full-hearted acceptance of self. For women today this means, above all, seeing ourselves as the expression of God seeking voice in our very femininity; being "women-identified women," not only "men-identified women," as the theologian Joan Chamberlain Engelsman is wont put it. For men, it means recognizing also, and cherishing finally, the hidden and culturally despised parts of themselves that give them access to solidarity with their sisters. It means allowing these aspects of themselves to be part of their self-identification, ministering through them.

This is, indeed, a new phenomenon, yet unexplored. For many of us, it is a frightening one. We prefer our silver hands. Religious life, for most of us, is *doing* oriented, and here our silver hands seem to have worked quite well — according to the structures identified for us. And that is certainly good. After all, the young miller's daughter was happy in her garden with her king. Yet is there not something unreal in all of this also, something incomplete, artificial, and unwholesome; something also that will finally bring misunderstanding and alienation; something that ultimately will drive some of us away? It seems to me that life in the Church as a whole and, by extension, life

among the religious who have given themselves to its service, is
lacking the "beauty which stems from the ensemble of our
strengths," from the full-bodied presence that comes from acceptance and celebration of our totality. Is not the dark forest of
diminishing membership and dying communities witnessing to
a need for something more — for greater depth, honesty, and
integrity; for an open-hearted and open minded questioning into
the why and who of our *being* rather than the mere concern with
our *doing*?

Von Franz interprets "living in the garden of the king" as
living "in accordance with collective standards," denying our
own capacity for self-determination; having our own inner attitudes and passions replaced "by an artificial one in which [we]
would do the right thing, because that is what's done"; behaving
"normally, but without spontaneity," our "valuable positive eros
quality" not fully alive.[9]

> Wherever [one] has an unredeemed demonic side ... all
> [one's] activities connected with the eros relationship
> ... will be performed in an artificial way. What cannot
> be produced spontaneously is brought about by force of
> will. ... There is insufficient spontaneity to produce in-
> stinctive action, and the silver hands have to replace those
> which have been cut off. Instinct is replaced by the rule
> of the collective. *But such people will be aware of a
> dead corner within them.*[10]

Ultimately, therefore, our psyche becomes restless again,
and we are driven out of our unredeemed artificiality into the
depth of loneliness and darkness. In the harshness and desola-

tion of our situation, however, if only we will recognize it and not psychologize or even theologize it away, lies our redemption. The symbol of the forest speaks to this experience. It could just as easily be a desert, an island in the sea, a top of a lonely mountain,[11] or even a dark night, as Sandra Schneiders sees it.[12] It is the place or the time when the ordinary becomes uncanny, the familiar strange. We retire then "into [our] own loneliness and must realize that . . . [we are] not yet really alive."[13]

It is my sense that, as religious, many of us are at the brink of this realization. Strangely, however, living by the rules of the king's garden remains widespread in religious congregations, and pro-forma events — where instinctive spontaneity must yield to "silver hands" — abound: We welcome prospective members and our associates almost universally with "silver hands," as we introduce them into our "prefab" programs and expect them to be happy in "our gardens." We prepare for chapters and discern leadership quite frequently that way also, as we refuse to recognize our "forced" spontaneity, even while evoking the guidance of the Holy Spirit, to whom we claim to abandon ourselves. We force personal budgets, in the name of "accountability," into straitjackets guarded by "silver hands." And all of us acquiesce, fully aware of the artificiality and deadness of it all.

Coming to the forest opens up a quite different and often disturbing experience. It unsettles us. It means reaching the "zero point where life is reduced to absolutely nothing"[14] and everything opens up to radical doubt. It means facing the unfamiliar and enduring the anxiety that this invariably evokes. It means feeling very alone most of the time, very "un-institutional" — "out of it," as some religious have described it to me. One feels unsupported and sorely tempted to retreat. A sister shared with me not long ago what might appear to be a trifling experience. To the contrary, however, it was both a painful and liberating moment for her and well illustrates "reaching the zero point" we are trying to understand here. Coming to an intersection in the road while driving to one of the many Saturday meetings at the motherhouse of her congregation, she suddenly found herself questioning what on earth was happening to her, and why she was doing this every Saturday without fail. "I sat there, frustrated, for a moment," she said, "to get in touch with all my guilt and feelings of obligation. Then I turned my car around, went home, and spent my afternoon planting flowers in the garden."

Institutionally, the "zero point" is often difficult to recognize, since we can easily distract ourselves with "escape techniques": pious chatter printed on newsprint, congregational studies, reports, questionnaires, and surveys — rehashing the old in the guise of the new. This is particularly hazardous when the distractions come through leadership's refusal to ask or to permit the painful questions and, thus, to point the way to interiority and transformation. Large congregations are often in greater danger here than small ones, since for them the dead weight of inertia is easier to hide and the busyness of administration can appear more relevant. Small groups, on the other hand, are more keenly aware of their own vulnerability and can more readily recognize artificiality and acknowledge their experience of desolation.

I remember saying to a large group of women religious who were virtually shutting down all avenues for welcoming new life in their area even as, in complete denial, they were praying for vocations: "Only if it hurts enough, will we change." Small groups are often hurting, and the *forest* is the "hurting enough." It is the "sickness unto death," the agony that brings with it depth listening, surrender, and the urgent mandate for change. And there, as von Franz puts it, "when there has been sufficient suffering,"[15] we finally are ready to meet the angel and are invited to enter into the little house deep in the darkness of the woods. "All who enter here shall be free," the inscription reads above the door. The handless maiden dwells there for seven years and, as she slowly learns to touch her inner core, her hands grow back, and she can reach out, once again, for what *she* treasures and touch what *she* loves.

On Becoming Rainmakers

In many respects, the ending of this tale echoes the story of the rainmaker with which I began my reflections on the vows in *Living the Vision*[16]: A withered old man comes to a community that has been extremely busy, but totally ineffective, in overcoming a drought. He has been called to help them, for they believe that he has extraordinary powers. To the surprise of everyone, he simply asks for a quiet little house where he shuts himself in for several days. Instead of working at bringing about rain outside, he focuses on his own inner harmony. Being in a disordered community where a great deal of energy is wasted in all kinds of distractions, he too finds himself scattered. He spends his time in the little house, therefore, reconnecting with the Tao and putting his inner self in order. In due time, the harmony from within effects harmony outside, and the drought ends.

This story, once again, links the individual or personal with the communal. It is important to note that the dark forest of suffering that we have been reflecting on, or the drought in the present example, do not primarily yield to group resolve per se. They are meant, first and foremost, for personal and individual transformation, affecting the body secondarily only through the members. In this time of crisis and destitution, therefore, it may be more accurate to understand the little house as designed for *each of us*, rather than for all of us collectively. Once again, we are reminded that the whole is in the part, and that personal conversion is primary to communal healing. Perhaps too many of us still expect congregational "fixatives" — position papers, corporate objectives, five-year plans designed for a better tomorrow. Like the drought-stricken community just mentioned, we too may be prolonging our plight because we are distracted and do not take responsibility for our own *inner harmony*.

It is becoming ever clearer to me that the realities of leadership and of administration in our congregations today do not necessarily coincide. Too often we expect both from the ones we elect, especially when we abdicate much of our own power to them. Might it not be, however, that authentic congregational renewal and the leadership that this requires lies in *each one of us assuming the responsibities of the rainmaker*? Our personal transformation needs, ultimately, to be the catalyst that helps our congregations to grow into wholesome and healthy communities. If our reflections on the "Need for 'Core' Involvement" in Part I are correct, we may need to deemphasize congregational projects somewhat and give ourselves some of our sparse free moments in order to reconnect with our inner core. We may need to reject accusations of "luxury" or "navelgazing" when religious choose to do this. Perhaps planting flowers in the garden is not such a bad idea.

The forest is the place of the "unconventional inner life. ... Living in the forest [means] sinking into one's innermost nature and finding out what it feels like."[17] For this, contact with nature can be very therapeutic. Von Franz maintains, in fact, that the feminine is profoundly linked to nature, and that reconnecting with one's neglected feeling function is often enhanced through contact with it. There is a simplicity in nature that does not demand the degree of differentiation that human relationships require.[18] Initial healing is, therefore, facilitated there.

Many of us today are forest dwellers, and the suffering required for individuation is often quite intense. We need space for this, re-creation time, but we also need love. Unfortunately few of us seem to have the honest support system that could help us realize that we are not alone, and that what we are experiencing is, in fact, healthy and actually necessary and transformative for our congregations as well. Much too often, therefore, we not only belittle, but also condemn ourselves, as we "take on" the catch-all defamation of "individualism," instead of realizing the importance of solitude for creative waiting, gestation, and individuation. Too frequently, also, collective standards still dominate us and, as a consequence, many of us feel not only guilty but also ever more isolated. "There is a natural process of growth, of maturing and transforming in the psyche. For a person who tries to act according to standards — to wait, to let things come, is sometimes the most difficult."[19]

It is difficult for a congregation also. We set timelines both for ourselves and for the individual members seeking professional help, as if healing, inspiration, and growth could be acquired like a college degree. Salvation cannot be preprogrammed. It is not ours to stipulate. The handless maiden was led into the forest's little dwelling *by an angel.* Sheer willpower will not grow our hands back, nor will it bring the rain — that can be accomplished *only by surrender, and the pain that this implies.*

The little house may not be the River Jabbock, but the seven years of dwelling within are a wrestling with God nonetheless.

Von Franz sees those who have lived the seven years of transformation as being marked by serenity and wisdom:

> By knowing so much about suffering, such people generally can readapt to life, and having gone through a great deal in a mature way, will naturally be able to help others. [They] will have something which attracts; for others will recognize [their] suffering, which will also make [them] more understanding. ... From now on the process [of growth] can continue, provided one is prepared to accept more suffering.[20]

We encounter here the requirements for ministry understood in its deepest sense. The hands that have grown back are not only symbolic of healing, but symbols *for* healing as well. With them we can reach beyond the functionality that "silver handedness" has imposed upon us and reach a hurting world. With them we can touch, once again, what is relevant and, having reconnected with the inner self that moves us beyond artificiality into the flesh-and-blood issues of life, we can embrace what needs loving and hold it toward wholeness.

Not long ago, while browsing through books at the airport, I came upon a quotation from Pierre Teilhard de Chardin. It has haunted me in the writing of this chapter, for it speaks so clearly of the task ahead: "The day will come when, after harnessing space, the winds, the tides and gravitation, we shall *harness for God the energies of love.* And on that day, for the second time in the history of the world, we shall have discovered fire."[21]

The harnessing of space and of the powers of the globe is surely a task well on the way. The harnessing of love energies lies yet before us. It is the task, I believe, of the "post modern era," as some call it. My name for it is the "next level of consciousness" for which, undoubtedly, the crisis we are experiencing at present is preparing us.[22] Our questions now are: How ready are we for this task, where can we start, and where do we need conversion?

The Call to Love

Myths and legends have a simple, almost innocent way of saying the complicated, the difficult to hear: A handless maiden spends seven years in the depths of a forest. During that time, her hands grow back and she becomes whole. Von Franz adds that in the process, she learns serenity and wisdom. It all seems quite lovely. Her young husband finds her and their child, and they live happily forevermore. Would that in real life the retrieving of affect — of our capacity to touch and hold, to cherish and care, to heal and nurture, and, ultimately, to be reunited to the contrasexual within — were quite that simple.

The symbolic interpretation of numbers sees "seven" as the symbol for pain,[23] and pain, indeed, is what movement into at-onement with one's self implies. There is a gradual softening of the heart over the span of years. The process is often excruciating. One is gentled through it, however, and slowly learns to embrace one's self from deep inside, where self-acceptance and utter brokenness meet and are called to face each other with uncompromising honesty. The embrace does not happen at will. It is often avoided for years, and quite unconsciously. It is talked about, seen as necessary for the world "out there," for others —

those to whom we minister — until finally the escape becomes impossible. Integrity confronts us as we face the task of connecting our own inner story with the Christ Event (the life, the death, the resurrection) and of surrendering to it as *our* existential truth. No one has spoken to this challenge better than Sebastian Moore: "To be changed," says he, "I need to be ... chased out of hating myself [or even loving myself exclusively] *in* another." Either of these attitudes can be understood as processes of "projection" that originate in self-estrangement; they are the reason for most wars, prejudice, violence, condemnation of others, and unhappiness in community life, but also of adulation and hero worship. In our story they are symbolized by silver-handedness — the inability to be *in touch* with one's self and with the world. For Sebastian Moore withdrawing projections, however, is not enough: I *must also* be "brought to seeing the self, that I hate, *as* other, as a man abandoned on a cross." I need to embrace Christ (who has taken on the sin and the vulnerability of humankind) as crucified in me. "I need to say '*there* is my life, my beauty, my possibility, my humanness, my full experience as a human, which is a personification of the universe, my outrageously ignored and neglected dream of goodness.'" I need to recognize and accept that "*that* welcomes me. That *means* me. That is my meaning. That is my symbol. That is my sacrament. That is my baptism. That is my bread and wine. That is my love."[24]

Conversion is at-onement with our deepest parts; withdrawing the evil we see in others and are blind to in ourselves; recognizing the blame, the excuses, for what they are; coming home, and loving ourselves; being Christified. And with this comes the serenity and the wisdom von Franz talks about; with this comes a soft heart, the capacity tenderly to hold and touch; with this comes compassion. "It changes our vision of reality." It challenges "our perception and our expectations not only of ourselves but also of others — of life itself."[25] As I pointed out in *Embraced by Compassion*: "The vision of compassion cuts through all boundaries. It is not shocked and does not easily take offense. It knows its own darkness, its own need of forgiveness, and having received mercy, it can now pass it on.[26]

Perhaps there is nothing more in need of the honest gaze of compassion for religious today than the very life we have *vowed* to live. Numerous books have been written in the last several years to invite us in that direction. As I have discussed in the first part of this book, however, it is my sense that many of us are still too anxious and, therefore, in denial regarding our life. We may read the books and even organize workshops, but our sharings tend to stop with pious exhortations and niceties printed out and summarized for all to ponder. We "process" ourselves out of, or away from, the "forest" in which so many of us are called to dwell at this time in our history; away from the confusion so many of us feel. We do not want to hurt anyone, or be hurt ourselves. Radical questions or views, however, can do that. Thus, whereas we may at times voice them in small groups, when we come to record or report our group sharing, we tend to "pietize" them into the palatable. They become pablum once again — easily digested, easily ignored.

Being Celibates Today

It is my sense that all three vows suffer from this lack of radical questioning. However, the vow that seems, perhaps, the most neglected in this way and the one most in need of liberation is our commitment to love within the context of consecrated celibacy. Situated squarely within the sexual taboo that has plagued Christianity ever since its earliest missionary endeavors in the Greco-Roman world, this vow remains to this day virtually unaddressed. Not that books and essays dealing with compulsory celibacy for diocesan priesthood are absent from today's literature. Nor are we missing historical accounts of Christianity's attitude toward sexuality. Many boldly point to the dualism that has colored our approach to our embodiment throughout our history. Some even deplore the harm that this has done. Our past's obsession with sexuality is well documented, therefore, but in the process of speaking about the coercion, the option *for* celibacy seems to remain almost totally "unreflected." Religious are, therefore, often left wondering whether their choice is in fact viable, healthy, and wholesome. There seems to be so much suffering and oppression associated with its history and so much rejection of celibacy, therefore, in contemporary society, that its power to call us into depth loving is completely obfuscated and its presence in our lives appears more like a cross than a grace.

Thomas C. Fox situates the topic well when he begins his reflection on celibacy with a description of American culture:

> In the United States, sex is practically a way of life. It is everywhere around us. It speaks to us and moves us. It drives motion pictures, cable television, magazines, fashions, cosmetics. Advertising uses sex to sell everything, from tobacco to automobiles, jeans to beer, mouthwash to refrigerators. It shapes our consciousness and unconsciousness. Madison Avenue knows this and invests

tens of billions each year to elicit sexual responses. Sex is used — and abused — in other ways too. The Federal Bureau of Investigation reports that pornography — not "soft" skin flicks shown in hotel chains, but the crude variety that features violence to women and exploits young children — is an $8 billion to $10 billion U.S. industry.

Step back for a moment and consider the vowed celibate. Imagine what it is like to live by the vow of celibacy in such an environment.[27]

Would it be surprising if religious felt intimidated, odd, for having taken this vow? Is it any wonder that some feel confused, that many seem to avoid dealing with the issue of celibacy and, at best, "endure" it, rather than consciously and creatively *living* the vow? They may not know how, in contemporary times, it can be explained or made sense of anyway. For many, it does not seem to make sense any longer either, and they may even feel "trapped" by it.

My experience is that some of our new members — the post–Vatican II vocations — are particularly vulnerable here. Somehow they want to enter into covenant with other women or men, to be about a common quest for the sake of the Gospel. Celibacy, they find out, is a requirement for this. Often they feel "saddled" with it, therefore, but not particularly "called" to it. Many, in their legitimate search for relationship and intimacy, are honestly struggling with what seems a confusing vow that is identified largely by "don'ts." They find it difficult to understand its purpose or value and often feel very alone and guilty in a congregation largely "mute" on this topic.

Readiness for the Choice

The women and men they meet in religious life today are, for the most part, "lifers" — those of us who entered in our late teens or early twenties, before Vatican II. We were, in many instances, too young for the profundity of our choice and had to grow into it over the years. Intimacy concerns and their sexual expression began to surface for us, therefore, only much later in life when obsessive supervision and mistrust became outmoded in religious communities. We were, however, often ill-equipped to deal with our new freedom. Some of us "acted out" initially during the freeing years of summer school programs in the sixties and early seventies. Many of our friends left religious life altogether. We remained — with a deeper appreciation of affect, I hope, but not necessarily with a better theology of celibacy. Some of us did not have the opportunity to "adolesce." From a state of dependence and childishness, we were often propelled into the vocabulary and concepts of interdependence and were expected to live by these without any adequate personal experience of maturation. Our psychosexual development was, therefore, frequently arrested for a long time. For many of us, guilt and confusion persist to this day.

Perhaps one of the most revealing testimonies of what I am attempting to address here is Francis B. Rothluebber's book, *Nobody Owns Me: A Celibate Woman Discovers Her Sexual Power.*[28] It is not my intention to analyze her testimony, from either a moral or psychological perspective. That, somehow, strikes me as irreverent and out of place. Rothluebber's story stands as a testament of woundedness healed. I do not believe it depicts or needs to be everyone's path. It speaks of one person's path, generously and courageously shared, and it ought to be respected as such. The book was brought to my attention during a lengthy discussion with a fellow religious — a spiritual director — who had asked my view concerning masturbation and sexual intimacy among religious. The struggle that Rothluebber discusses in her work seemed very honest to my colleague, and I surmise that it is also quite widespread.

It seems that an honest and compassionate look at sexual needs and behavior vis á vis celibacy frequently opens up numerous questions that may initially move us beyond the morality of our tradition and invite us rather into the realm of human development and maturation. Masturbation may be a case in point. I can think of nothing wiser than to help the often quite guilt-ridden individual inquiring about it to focus *around* the issue rather than *on* it: "When do I masturbate; what triggers the need?" "What do the fantasies around the experience tell me about myself, my desires, my needs, my hopes, my dreams, my relationships?" "What does masturbation do for me — does it uplift me, relax me; does it depress or haunt me? If so, why? Does it free me or imprison me? How?" "Is my need for it increasing or decreasing?" "How does masturbation help or hinder my relational skills?" Unless issues of psychosexual development are dealt with, morality cannot be addressed meaningfully. Its precepts may be known, but it oppresses and debilitates rather than guides human behavior. It imposes itself on, rather than growing out of, our experience. The issue of masturbation needs to be looked at within this context.

It has long been my view that the Catholic propensity to give answers to questions before they are asked, to ask for commitments before these are developmentally possible (infant baptism best symbolizes this), tends to turn the normal maturation process upside-down and, at times, may cause more harm, especially in the area of guilt, than it does good. As far as celibacy generally is concerned, I do believe the question needs at least to be asked *how* something as intrinsic a part of our being as human genital expression can be renounced responsibly if it has not been honestly addressed and truly understood. If this is what, in fact, has happened to a large number of religious, and avoidance rather than openness has been our approach, it ought not be surprising that in many instances the depth dimension of this vow has been thoroughly obfuscated. Growth into it may have been prevented and, with it, the sexual awareness of the person who chose it prematurely. This problem may also have been exacerbated by the prudishness and obsessive negativity demonstrated toward sexuality in general on the part of much of the Christian/Catholic world. It created an environment of secrecy and suspicion in convents and monasteries, where honest questions were silenced and healthy affection stifled. It operated in an atmosphere of "otherworldliness," of abstract spirituality that was "dissociated from the body, life, earth and social relationship."[29] It fostered a type of disembodiment and all the lovelessness, insecurity, coldness, and weariness that are connected with, and hide behind, abstraction.[30] It wounded many of us.

There were, of course, always some among us with a healthier and a growth-enabling experience of religious life. Perhaps they came from less sexually compulsed family or educational settings; perhaps they entered later and had worked through their adolescence. For them, vowed celibacy may, no doubt, have had its struggles, its learning moments, its disappointments and painful relationships. Somehow they were able, however, consciously to embrace their bodies and live *through* them. Thus they experienced breakthroughs that deepened their personality, either "feminizing" or "masculinizing" it accordingly. Nevertheless, even for them, the sexually hostile environment of religious life frequently was hurtful. Quite often, if breakthroughs could not be had with discretion (that is in secret, accompanied with all the contortions that the need for privacy necessitates in a convent or monastery setting), religious rarely had the chance to reevaluate their choices, reflect on their behavior, learn from it, and come to a mature celibate lifestyle on their own. The decision was, instead, made for them by the "competent" authority, and often they were advised to leave the congregation.

It is a fact worth considering that in many religious congregations to this day, the strict adherence to constitutional dicta regarding the other two vows is rarely enforced punitively. The "violations" against celibacy, however, are seen as clear and precise: according to our tradition, always serious — mortally sinful. They are often dealt with severely and with no seeming knowledge of, or respect for, the growth *process* necessary for a mature appropriation of the value of celibacy, without which any meaningful commitment is impossible. Nor is relegating this process summarily to the years of "formation" the answer. This is done, nevertheless, all too often today. It clearly exhibits our lack of understanding even now of human sexuality, of embodiment, of psychosexual development, as well as of our own growth needs in this regard. Anyone who visualizes the movement into celibacy as fitting neatly into a timeline, does not understand it and has probably not gone through it herself or himself.

The Vow That Defines Us

Celibacy, no doubt, holds a special place in religious life. It is the distinguishing mark of our consecration, and, understandably, our being able to embrace its value is uniquely important for our life. Sandra Schneiders states this well:

> For two reasons consecrated celibacy is unique among vows professed by religious. First, it is the only vow whose content has been a constant factor in all forms of religious life throughout history. From the time of the consecrated virgins and widows of the first century to our own day religious life has always involved a commitment to lifelong celibacy. Second, celibacy is the only one of the three vows whose object is, strictly speaking, an evangelical "counsel" in the sense that it is a response to an invitation not addressed to all Christians. Although poverty and obedience are structured differently in the life of a religious than they are in the life of a married or single Christian, religious are certainly not the only Christians to whom the evangelical challenges of poverty of spirit and obedience to God are addressed. Consecrated celibacy, in other words, is the defining characteristic of religious life.[31]

The tragedy lies precisely in the fact that not only for the culture, but also for religious themselves, the *point* and *purpose* for celibacy has become questionable. It desperately needs to be rescued from the ruins of dualism and spiritualism to be revisioned and contextualized.

We do not give up the genital expression of love because it

is "better and more godly to live in virginity, or in the unmarried state than to marry," in spite of what Trent teaches,[32] or what exulted percentage of salvation Thomas Aquinas attributes to virginal individuals.[33] Some of us are all too familiar with vocational triumphalism from as far back as our high school "vocation rallies" and their three "states of perfection." Hierarchism was ingrained in the Catholic system and is difficult to shed. Well into this century the rewards for celibacy were situated there. Philip Sheldrake speaks to this clearly:

> In defining holiness, an outstanding priority in western Christianity has been what may be called the *clerical-monastic* one, that is "special ways" as opposed to the Christian life as a whole. From the early centuries of the Church, the development of a hierarchy and the differentiation of charisms gradually set apart those who had chosen the "better part" or who were deemed more whole-hearted in their discipleship — in practice the clerics and celibates-ascetics. Such elitism was also related to a priority of "spiritual" over "material" reality, often linked to a suspicion of human sexuality... .
>
> The first language of Christian perfection was that of martyrdom. ... The emergence of monasticism ... continued the martyr model of holiness and developed it from victory over physical death to victory over the world as death-dealing. ... [M]onasticism, not inherently but effectively, abandoned the idea of perfection for the ordinary Christian. Thus a division was created within the Church between the perfect and the imperfect, symbolized by physical withdrawal.[34]

None of us are strangers to this account. For many of us, for the major part of our religious life, celibacy was indeed the vow that held the "distinction" of setting us apart. By it we committed ourselves to a plethora of physical "don'ts," which somehow gave us an aura of self-abnegation and ushered us into the dualistic hierarchy of spiritual elitism. Celibacy, it was said, "freed" us for the reign of God, detached us from binding loves, and allowed us to wander where others could not go. It was celibacy that opened for us, in a very special way, the realm of the spirit.

But what happens when this attitude of dualism finds itself surrounded by a theology that is steadily moving toward a more holistic approach to life? What do we do with our spiritual separatism in the face of the profound recognition of the sacredness of our incarnation that is rapidly taking hold of a growing number of us and has us see abstinence for the sake of abstinence (placing the spiritual over the physical) as suspect, even unhealthy; as psychologically damaging and unsound? What is left, in other words, when the hatred and fear of our embodiment evaporates; when rejection of matter, and of the sexuality that symbolizes it, is no longer a sign of perfection; when the dualistic foundations for a spirituality of celibacy are shaken, and the vow within this context appears triumphalistic, shallow, even sterile? Are there any reasons why celibacy should then be embraced? Can traditional motivations be, in fact, recontextualized — revisited, as it were — and authenticated in a spirituality relevant way for today?

Why Celibacy Today?

Sandra Schneiders, in her characteristic clarity, identifies a variety of traditional as well as present-day explanations and motivations for celibacy. "Religious celibacy has been explained," she says, "as marriage to Christ, freedom for contemplation or for the ministry, eschatological witness, countercultural stance, or condition for prophetic community life."[35] It is my sense that any one of these is worth consideration, provided it is rightly understood and identified as one's *personal* motivation rather than as a *general principle*.

What seems primary here, and essential to a holistic paradigm for spirituality, is the importance of rejecting every attempt at identifying and absolutizing any one explanation and motive as normative for Christian perfection generally. In order for each to be relevant and genuinely meaningful to us, all triumphalism needs to be avoided. What is a way to God is not necessarily *the* way to God. What is good for one is not necessarily good for all, nor is any walk of life higher than or above all the others. Thus, because a celibate lifestyle allows *some* believers greater freedom for ministry or contemplation, it is not a foregone conclusion that *all* of us would benefit that way. Christian ministry, as we all know, is effectively carried out by numerous married ministers, both ordained and nonordained. Their generosity and talent is in every way a match for the nonmarried. When one's call to live out one's baptism is through sacramental matrimony, one's ministry will blossom through this call as well. Our baptismal consecration allows for a diversity of vocations. The capacity for ministry and personal holiness is in accordance to one's faithfulness to these.

Freedom for Ministry

Now, when "freedom for ministry" (the ascetical/apostolic understanding, as Schneiders discusses it) is the primary motivation for celibacy, the latter seems to be understood as a means toward an end rather than as an end in itself. Clearly, here the end is "seen as more global than non-marriage itself, but as fostered in some important way by celibacy."[36] One holds that the way one has chosen to live, and what one feels called to do, is enhanced by this vow: "The ends which celibacy has been undertaken to foster include the life of prayer or contemplation, ministry, community life of the kind that would be difficult or impossible among married members, and various kinds of witness that can be given more easily by an unmarried person."[37]

In the situation described here, the individual feels called to the apostolate and to a life of prayer in community. She or he sees the way of celibate love as *enabling* this kind of life for her or him. In this sense, celibacy is embraced as a "gift." It may be important to note in this context, however, that the choice to embrace celibacy and to live it with integrity does not necessarily come easily. This is not, therefore, how the term "gift" or "charism" should be understood. Nor ought the aversion to things sexual be misconstrued as "gift" and, therefore, as proof of a religious vocation. It can be quite the contrary. I personally have difficulty with the term "gift" with respect to celibacy, precisely because it can be so misleading, especially when it is used to negate difficulty. It seems to me that it is too often spoken glibly. This is particularly unfortunate when it is tied to the mandatory celibacy of ordination. Few, I believe, can expect to embrace this vow without pain and sacrifice. It is an asceticism. We may be called to it, but the call does not necessarily facilitate the choice. What is required is mature discipline and a life of prayer and of integrity.

Spiritual Marriage

Of special interest to me is the explanation for celibacy that Sandra Schneiders mentions first: She identifies "a very small number of contemporary religious" who embrace "consecrated virginity understood in a mystical/nuptial way as marriage to Christ." Non-marriage is seen here as "the form of total personal dedication to Jesus, just as marriage is the form of life-long personal dedication to another human being."[38] Here again, the choice to live in faithfulness to the grace of "spiritual marriage" *through celibacy* is a deeply and uniquely personal one, but not a necessary one. Nor is the phenomenon of mystical marriage restricted to Christianity or Catholicism. John Ferguson attests that it, in fact, "is frequent in mystics of all religions."[39]

My own fascination with this phenomenon stems partially from the fact that, though it is relatively rare today, I personally have been graced just in the last few years with the acquaintance of three women who have experienced union with God in

this way. Only one is a religious and understands her vocation
in the manner discussed above. The second woman, single but
not a consecrated virgin, was unchurched in her youth. Interest
in religion was virtually nonexistent in her family. She became
a highly qualified professional, but yearnings for a deeply spiritual life began to grow in her over the years and escalated to the
point where she could no longer function meaningfully in her
field. She started to read and study religion, submitted herself
to the spiritual guidance of professionals, and, after much discernment, joined the Episcopalian church. She now lives as an
anchorite. Her experiences have been both those of intense suffering and of deep joy. The Song of Songs is truly her story.

The third woman of my acquaintance is a mother of five, a
happily married woman whose call to mystical marriage pre-
ceded any understanding of such a phenomenon. She is a deeply
religious person and, whenever her busy family schedule permits, she goes off for a few days of quiet. During one of these
days a few years ago, the "call of the Bridegroom" overwhelmed
her. She was, of course, greatly puzzled by this experience and
took a while to work out its meaning with the help of spiritual
direction and guidance. Eventually, she and her husband entered the Catholic Church. She lives out her union with God as
a married woman to this day.

In the experience of mystical marriage, God most frequently
is seen as Bridegroom, and the soul as bride. Celibacy can be a
fitting response to this experience, and the history of Christianity certainly attests to this choice on the part of many of the
giants of our tradition. The preceding examples show once again,
however, that the celibate response to this experience is not the
only possible one (nor the one "par excellence"). The union is

of a *mystical/spiritual nature.* It is clear, therefore, that responses to it can vary, and that *all* descriptions of it will fall short and can only be by analogy. Quite frequently, in fact, metaphors are mixed and even confused as one attempts to describe the un-speakable intimacy experienced:

There is a fascinating passage from Teresa de Jesus's *Conceptions of the Love of God* in which she oscillates between God as husband, wife and mother: "When this most opulent Spouse is pleased to enrich and more emi-nently to caress souls, He so converts them into Himself that, as a person swooning through excessive delight and pleasure, the soul seems to herself to be suspended in those divine arms and to rest on that divine side and those divine breasts; and does nothing but enjoy, being sustained with divine milk with which her Spouse goes feeding her. ... She sees herself ... caressed by Him who knows how and is able to do it; she does not know what to compare it to, except the caress of a mother who loving her baby tenderly, nurses and fondles him in this way."[40]

The mystical nature of this experience and its rarity, as well as the sometimes confusing language with which it is described, may quite readily contribute to a contemporary lack of under-standing of it. The low tolerance for it among some religious today may also spring, however, from memories of the unre-flective and often sentimental use of its symbolism for entrance ceremonials in their religious congregations. Sandra Schneiders speaks to these accurately:

The use of bridal gowns and veils in reception and profession ceremonies, of marital euphemisms in the
sections of rules and constitutions dealing with the vow
of chastity, and of sentimental spousal language in
spiritual literature, because it did not reflect the real
experience of most religious, was seen as superficial at
best and offensive at worst. Few religious today are
comfortable with nuptial language about religious
commitment, partly because it does not reflect their experience and partly because of the memory of its use in
times past. Again, it is unfortunate that this historical
development has deprived those whose experience of
virginity is indeed nuptial of symbolism and language
that would be genuinely expressive for them. In fact,
the mystical/nuptial language has been preserved in the
literature of mysticism where it continues to nourish
those who can understand from their own experience
what is being described.[41]

Although few of us may be able to relate to bridal mysticism as the reason for our acceptance of the vow of celibacy, the
life we have embraced, nevertheless, provides us with a remark-
able opportunity, in a barren and aching culture, to bear witness
to the primacy of all of humanity's initial as well as final God-
directedness. The non-coupled lifestyle and our renunciation
of progeny marks us. In a culture where gratification is the
norm, consecrated celibacy stands for doing without, for
God-dependency, for looking deeper, for waiting, for vigilance,
and for another kind of fulfillment. Celibate loving, regardless

of how empowering it may be in its freedom for ministry, ultimately speaks of aloneness and longing. It can bring us depth, wholeness, and happiness, no doubt. But as it draws us, over the span of a lifetime, ever more deeply into the love that alone can fill our heart's desire, "it will also, and inexorably, lead us through loneliness into [a] 'final solitude,'" where inevitably it will lay open "the radical insufficiency of all human loving and reveal us to ourselves as the living symbols of all of humanity's ultimate and ontological homesickness for God."[42] A powerful call, this; an extraordinary opportunity! The question remains: Do we as religious today — *can* we — seize it? Is the countercultural stance — the eschatological, prophetic witness — *in fact* truly ours? Do religious today stand as beacons pointing into the heart of God? Is our life vibrant enough to make our "doing without" a credible symbol? How do we embrace our sexuality today? How do we work out our relational and affective needs realistically?

A Countercultural Stance
Thomas Fox, as I mentioned earlier (Part II, "The Call to Love"), makes it clear that we live in an age of promiscuity. The very extremes that dualism fostered on the side of the spiritual and in favor of detachment bordering on angelism have received in our times the go-ahead for licentiousness. Sexual gratification is the dessert, if not the main course, for almost any casual encounter on the TV screens in our homes. It is generally viewed as *the* way by which love is measured and evaluated and is accepted overall as "only normal." Given this situation, it seems difficult to deny that genital abstinence in an environment of sexual laissez-faire will be interpreted as countercultural. But,

whereas what is countercultural has great potential for being prophetic, it need not necessarily be so. It can also appear as senseless, as meaningless, as abnormal, as sick. *For the countercultural to be prophetic it needs to emerge from a healthy, credible, happy, and wholesome source. It needs to exude balance and flow from self-esteem and inner conviction.* That much of the latter is missing among religious today is, I believe, beyond debate.

I have suggested already that many of us, caught up in our culture and in its values (albeit often unconsciously), are only minimally able to critique its dicta. There is a tendency, therefore, to feel apologetic, even embarrassed and confused, about our celibate way of life. Some of us, in fact, may actually feel like victims, caught (confusingly enough, by our own choosing) in a dehydrated communal lifestyle where love has been reduced to decency — if that — and where those who dare to be friends are more often than not criticized rather than empowered. We feel emotionally deprived in a gathering of professionals, busy about many things but seemingly incapable of touching each other in meaningful and healing ways. Many of us may want to point to our commitment to celibacy (rather than to the lack of depth per se in our lives) as the primary reason for our emotional impoverishment.

It is, of course, not difficult to understand how emotional deprivation can lead to compulsive and unhealthy as well as damaging behavior patterns. It paves the way for shallow emotional involvements that we drift into or out of in Don Juan style whenever the pain gets too intense. We collect friendships to fill up our emptiness. We embrace a honeymoon mentality that has us meet each other for the occasional sharing session and support group, but protects us from the pain of loving the other in our sinfulness and from facing the dysfunctionality that appears only in the blood, sweat, and tears of daily coexistence. Finally, we move to complete withdrawal of affect in order to avoid the suffering that sustained encounter invariably brings with it. Escape, however, as I see it, is not the word for the credible celibate of today, nor is dispassion. Several years ago I attempted to establish a viable reason and explanation for celibacy by stressing the relation between covenantal love in community and our celibate commitment. I found support for this position in the numerous observations to this effect voiced in the sections dealing with celibacy in the revised constitutions of religious congregations throughout this country. It seemed to me that the excessive emphasis on "holy detachment" of the past had given way in these documents to *loving*. The constitutions of my own congregation say it well. They speak of consecrated chastity "as our way of loving and being loved. ... Because of our covenant with one another, we rejoice in the richness and strength of our friendships. We support one another in community ... and we choose to relate to all in ways that nurture life."[43] Other constitutions word things differently but speak to the same general recognition that our baptismal call to witness to love, our covenant with one another, and our vow of celibacy are intimately connected.

One can draw great encouragement from such statements. They manifest vision and a movement into a much deeper acceptance of religious women and men as whole persons. They speak of the longing that, in many respects, inspired this vision. They witness to a relationality that is much needed in our time. They also present a frontier that yet needs exploration; a challenge for us that is yet, in many respects, unrealized in our midst. I believe that if celibacy is to open up for us the grace that loving one another with authenticity holds in store for us, we will need to accept intimacy — its power and its pain — as part of our lives. We will need to learn about trust and commitment, discipline and self-gift; about perseverance and faithfulness, and passion. Celibacy today, celebrated and lived healthily, needs to embrace the flow of sexual energy, to acknowledge it as good — as essential, in fact, to our incarnation. It needs to channel this energy with intent into the numerous creative and life-giving forms of loving that cry out for expression in our love-starved world.

The Transmutation
of Energy

It is my growing conviction that the meaningfulness of celibacy and its witness value in the post-dualistic, post-modern world beckoning us will be found increasingly in the transmutation and channeling of energy; in cosmic connectedness and responsibility; in an open, heartfelt acceptance of, and witnessing to, the holiness of all of creation. Few have written more significantly on this topic of late than has Gerald G. May, M.D.[44]

Referring to both Eastern and Western contemplative traditions, May posits a common-ground energy as the foundational life-force of the universe, from which all the diverse manifestations of love present in the cosmos derive their power. The human being, as the "cosmos grown to consciousness,"[45] is the *locus* where this life-force is processed "in varying ways and degrees," and where it finds expression. What Augustine intuited already in his time as love but made holistically difficult to access due to his separation of spirit and matter, Eastern traditions to this day call *chi, ki, Sacti* and effectively use both for healing (as in acupuncture) as well as in *tai chi* and *aikido*. "Eastern thought generally views this energy as synonymous with basic life-force," May tells us. He says that, aside from existing "within the physical bodies of people," it also "forms patterns of dynamic interrelationship among all things in the universe." It is manifest in all phenomena, including human emotions. "Sexual feelings, anger, pleasure, hope, and fear are all seen as expressions of this universal energy, manifested within awareness in very specific ways." Our mental activity expresses it also, but emotions do so most obviously. "Emotions are both experientially and philosophically associated with drive, liveliness, and motivation." They are, therefore, "the clearest examples of intrapsychic manifestations of universal energy."[46] In the human being — specifically in human consciousness — the differentiation, classification, and subsequent moral judgment on the use and expression of this energy takes place. In us, therefore, its channeling, guiding, and transmutation is made possible. According to May, meditative practices in particular can bring this about. They enable depth response, creativity, and freedom in areas that too frequently have been interpreted as beyond human control.

The Contemplative Stance

In order to exemplify what he means by the multiplicity of emotional expressions through which this basic, rather diffuse, and all-pervasive life energy is processed and ultimately becomes manifested and focused, May cites what appears to be a lengthy journal entry of a woman he identifies merely as a "Roman Catholic nun." He suggests that her many years of quiet prayer and meditation, as well as her training in the field of psychology, well prepared her for experiencing this channeling of energy. It also gave her the equanimity and releasement to encounter her feelings in peace, without condemnation or compulsion. This in turn allowed her the freedom not to let herself be overwhelmed by them:

> I went into the retreat with my mind filled with busyness. I was depressed and angry about some of my relationships at work, and I was even more distressed by some sexual feelings which had begun to stir within me in relation to a man I had to work closely with. I have had such feelings before, and I can usually handle them without difficulty. But this time they seemed stronger and more tenacious, and they were proving to be quite a distraction. My daily prayer time had been filled with thoughts about work and images of this man, and it seemed I couldn't get beyond those superficialities to any true sense of quiet. I had lost touch with the quiet center of spirit which is such an important "home" for me. I was indeed feeling ready for a retreat.
>
> During the first part of the retreat my mind remained highly turbulent, but after many hours of just sitting with all the mental noise, things began to quiet down. The multiplicity of thoughts and images which had preoccupied my attention began to disappear. As they left, I became aware of another layer of turbulence beneath them, *this consisting of emotions.*
>
> Watching this very quietly, *I experienced the whole gamut of emotions* coming through my mind one after another as if on a parade. *Sadness, anger, frustration, sexual desire, guilt, fear, hope, and now and then some peace, lightness, and humor.* First I recognized all of

these feelings, much like body sensations *but coming from deep within my awareness. They seemed to originate very deeply,* and for a while I became fascinated with seeing how they came into being. *It appeared that something lay behind these feelings — some origin or source — and that my usual experience of them had been very superficial.* As I moved more intimately towards that point of origin, it seemed as if there was a level at which a kind of *diffuse dynamic "percolation" was taking place. Indeed, this appeared to be at a very primeval point,* perhaps at that place where the mind and the body truly meet. I know I lost all ability to discriminate between what was mental and what physical.

Out of this level of "percolation" there seemed to come spurts of activity which became attached to certain mental concepts or words or memories or images. When this attachment took place, I could immediately identify that "spurt" or "spark" as a feeling; an emotion. And with just a little more discrimination I could label the feeling as anger or sadness or whatever. *I was left with the conviction that what I experience as emotions on a day-to-day basis is really just a superficial interpretation of a much larger and more generalized process. More importantly I was deeply impressed by the fact that while all this activity takes place it is possible for some kind of awareness to be present, totally unruffled, watching it all with complete serenity.* There is something deeply reassuring about that.[47]

It seems to me that this account speaks with particular relevance to persons who vow celibacy. Emotions of all kinds including sexual feelings, experienced within the context of one's life, are presented here as outgrowths of something much larger and deeper, something that frequently cannot be reached and often remains hidden or unknown due to premature foreclosure. These emotions, we are told, can be observed "with complete serenity." They are premoral, a manifestation of primordial energy bubbling up in us, who are the place where love comes to consciousness, is channeled and expressed.

When, during my workshops on the vows, I address sexual arousal — especially the seemingly gender-irrelevant arousal that catches a person by surprise during a spontaneous expression of affection or even during prayer — I often suggest that one simply "take note of it with interest" rather than react to it with fear or guilt. It is claimed that the very disposition that allows something to *be* (without *reacting to it* or *acting on it)*, frees the experience, which is then viewed simply as a *phenomenon* — something that appears and gives itself over for our contemplation. This approach liberates us, furthermore, from wanting to take responsibility for something that has appeared *from beyond our freedom* and is merely revealing its presence and bringing itself to our awareness. It puts us into a contemplative stance even as we continue our usual activities. It fosters self-reflection and, therefore, can teach us much about ourselves and the nature of loving — matters otherwise obscured by misplaced self-condemnation.

The Danger of Obsessive Control

Western Christianity is, of course, not very familiar with such an approach, especially in the area of sexual stimulation, where everything has for too long been interpreted as sinful. The fostering of obsessive control and denial, as well as of scrupulous self-examination and suspicion, has been widespread in our tradition. A contemplative attitude toward one's sexual impulses and feelings was unheard of. These were "dirty" feelings and "dirty" thoughts, and anyone in whose company one might get them was "a near occasion of sin" and had to be avoided. That the very preoccupation and fear associated with sexual urges intensified rather than ameliorated them never seemed to occur to anyone. Therapists today call it "anticipatory anxiety," and Viktor Frankl, among others, suggests that it brings about precisely what the individual fears so much.[48] He suggests the logotherapeutic technique known as "paradoxical intention" as a viable response. It operates within the context of "self-detachment" and utilizes the self-observation toward which the meditative stance we are discussing is so well disposed:

> A phobic person usually tries to avoid the situation in which his [her] anxiety arises, while the obsessive-compulsive tries to suppress, and thus to fight, his [her] threatening ideas. In either case the result is a strengthening of the symptom. Conversely, if we succeed in bringing the [person] to the point where he [she] ceases to flee from or to fight his [her] symptoms ... then we may observe that the symptoms diminish and that the [person] is no longer haunted by them.[49]

Seeing Emotions as Events

May insists that nonattachment enables us to recognize emotions as *events* rather than qualities. It gives us the space that allows us to observe what is going on within, without becoming overwhelmed by it. Difficult as this may be, May insists that it can be enhanced through practice.[50] The breathing techniques and deep centering prayer experiences that so many religious practice nowadays can be of great help here. In "contemplative insight," one simply gives oneself over to the nonmanipulative observation of whatever presents itself and lets it be.

Once we can see emotions and feelings as events that emerge into awareness from "a root substratum of raw energy," their power over us lessens:

> [T]hey can be viewed as temporary expressions of an energy that has been differentiated, labeled, and manifested in certain specific ways. And whether the emotions stay in awareness or disappear, whether they enlarge or fade, elaborate or simplify, there is a constant capacity to notice the field of awareness within which they occur. This field of awareness is a steadfast and enduring bedrock that need never be influenced or altered by the drama and turbulence of emotional play. From this secure foundation, all the machinations of mind can be seen as play, and one is free to choose what, if anything, to attend to.[51]

"Isn't this interesting? I am feeling sexually aroused," the celibate says to herself or himself as she or he hugs a companion or thinks of someone dear, and then she or he cheerfully

moves on in the conversation or activity at hand. It is not necessary to tense up or withdraw. One does not resolve never to
touch or contact the other again, for she or he is not a near occasion of sin, but simply someone through whose nearness life
energy bubbled up in us in the form of arousal. We simply take
note of this, recognize that we are fully alive, and let it be.
Releasement of this kind prevents the intensification of feelings
that excessive attention would have brought about. May, agree-
ing with Frankl, explains this as follows:

> In a situation where one is immediately aware of a feel-
> ing coming into awareness and chooses not to do any-
> thing with it except watch, it seems that the energy of
> the emotion bursts within the field of consciousness like
> a fire-flash in darkness, growing to brilliance and then
> fading instantaneously. Here the energy is neither re-
> pressed nor elaborated upon. Since nothing is done to
> or with it, it simply sparkles into awareness and is gone.[52]

Seeing emotions simply as emerging manifestations of energy can shed light on confusion both in the area of sexuality as
well as spirituality. The initial stimulus for either one can readily
result in feelings associated with the other one.[53] One can feel
deep spiritual union during coitus; one can also feel sexually
stimulated during prayer. The reason for this lies in confusion
around the nature of longing and the yearning for fulfillment,
"but also [in] primary misdirections in the processing of emotional energy."[54] Given the irrelevance of the initial stimulus, it
is possible to conclude that environment, past experiences, fantasies, habitual inclinations, and personality, to mention but a

few, all play a role in how the root energy becomes manifest.[55] May gives the example of a waterfall to illustrate this. When a silent retreatant comes upon it, it may enhance his or her prayerfulness. A pair of lovers on an evening walk may, on the other hand, find it deeply romantic. We can all think of less innocent examples: What makes one weep drives another to violence. What evokes humor in one brings out anger in another. What may appear totally unrelated can evoke a completely unexpected erotic response.

We live in a mindless age where awareness of inner stirrings and self-observation are virtually nonexistent. Emotions are, therefore, rarely observed in their beginnings and are full-blown and "beyond the scope of personal influence" well before we are even aware of them. Thus, we become their victims in many respects, and choosing our behavior in relation to them becomes difficult. The notion of "emotional freedom" is virtually an anomaly today. Somehow we have come to believe that "venting" our feelings is freedom — that letting them all flow out "liberates" us.

Yet the meditative experiences May recounts in his book present another picture: We read there about "sinking into deeper and deeper levels of [one's] mind," and encountering there layers upon layers of feelings; of going into these feelings and of finally encountering, deep below them all, "a longing and a loving so immense that it almost terrifie[s]." With this encounter and its silent embrace comes a sense of liberation — a realization that feelings do not impede our freedom to be who we are; that feelings, ultimately, "are just feelings."[56] Few of us may experience such depth in this day and age. Maybe we are afraid of being terrified. I cannot help wondering, however, whether perhaps the secret of celibate freedom and its witness value in our time lies *there*.

Years ago in his classic work, *The Idea of the Holy,* Rudolf Otto spoke at length of the element of "energy" encountered in depth experiences of the holy. He suggested that it "clothes itself" in a number of "symbolic expressions," among them: "vitality, passion, emotional temper, will, force, movement, excitement, activity, impetus."[57] Our tradition has in many respects, of course, preferred to nullify this holy power within, speaking of it in terms of the static, the unmoved mover. As such it has contributed to the rationalization that has prevented us from encountering our deepest center and the Holy One there. It has kept religion in the head and seen feelings as base and unholy.

Perhaps it is time for us today to embrace once again the wholeness that we are and to surrender to the energy of the holy as it gives itself to us. Perhaps we are being called to a much deeper level — to open ourselves up to the encounter with the "force that knows not stint nor stay, which is urgent, active, compelling and alive."[58] Perhaps the time is ripe for our liberation from our rationalizations and dualisms and, paradoxically, also from our mindlessness. Perhaps contemplative presence to ourselves, though it initially may terrify us, will nevertheless open for us heretofore hidden sources of life and love and meaning.

Encountering Our Sexuality

For some religious, the invitation to encounter their own sexuality, to work *with* sexual feelings and urges rather than *against* them, seems not only a relatively new idea, but also an unnerving proposition. Years of dualistic training have severed a good number of us quite thoroughly from the deep energy centers of our own embodiment and make what we have reflected on previously extremely difficult. We may, therefore, be intellectually stimulated by holistic theories, but in our interpersonal relationships we tend to flee them. We prefer to play it safe. Detachment has helped us through the years to stay cool. We are, therefore, polite, even friendly, but distant. We may have many friends, but none that are close enough to hurt us. Our own passions are denied, hidden well both from ourselves and from others. We have kept them securely at bay. The experience of passionate involvement in all respects is inappropriate, we feel, for our celibate lifestyle, and channeling energy seems foreign to us. Although we claim we have nothing against intimacy and friendship, we treat any manifestation of it in our midst with suspicion. Somehow we believe in "universal intimacy." Since we call ourselves sisters or brothers, we assume it is possible for all of us to love one another equally. That even Jesus seemed to have had special friends totally escapes us. In fact, we claim to love people "in the name of Jesus" — a kind of passionless experience that avoids involvement and is seemingly oblivious to the fact that it is rarely appreciated by anyone. We are polite, even kind. We never interrupt or disagree openly with those around us. We speak the appropriate words at the right time and avoid all conflictual situations. We never stay anywhere long enough to get involved. When life becomes relationally charged and emotionally difficult, we quote Scripture, proclaim ourselves a "pilgrim people," and move on. We lack the passion of our embodiment and are out of touch with the sacredness of our incarnation. Instead of living our celibacy, we have probably avoided it. Hence we also have difficulty truly experiencing the presence of God and the life-force in creation. God's absence has never been felt, either. Jesus may be present in the Eucharist for us, but, often without even being aware of it, we fail to touch him and feel him in one another, let alone in ourselves. Although most of our charisms laud hospitality, our convents or friaries are sterile and private places rather than welcoming homes. We lack the passion of true life. With respect to sexual feelings and urges, we do not seem to have or acknowledge any — they have been denied long ago, and talk of them generally makes us nervous and uncomfortable.

For others among us the dualism of our past has spawned the opposite reaction, albeit sometimes late in life. We have come to know the energy that flows deep within us and through us and exult in its expression. Passion is not foreign to us anymore, nor is it feared. We may, at times, however, be quite unaware of its force and power. Thus, we may lack a healthy respect for it and can easily be overwhelmed by it. Because of past prohibitions, we now seek to "express ourselves." When someone speaks of *channeling* energy, therefore, we may not immediately find ourselves interested. We hear "control, denial, repression" instead, and react to this in the "over–against" stance elicited by old, rejected tapes. Some of us want to allow ourselves to "experience it all." We are the children of our culture. We rationalize our excesses with speeches about liberation and health, and can easily forget the responsibility that humanizes our energies. We speak of the "fundamental right to pleasure," but want to avoid the pain that accompanies all human loving. Our passion, though we feel it, is not always grounded in the integrity of incarnate spirits, hence it too may be shallow and may lack substance. Our newfound liberalism tends to rush us to foreclose on our experiences. "It's got to be right, because it feels so good," often becomes our criterion as we mistake ardor for sacredness.

Sexual Awakening

Several years ago during one of my seminars on women's issues, a newer member of a large religious congregation identified herself to me as lesbian and shared also that in her congregation she belonged to a lesbian support group. During our sessions, we had touched upon the flow of masculine and feminine energy, and her meeting with me was prompted by the desire for clarification in this area and her need to relate the material to her friendship and intimacy needs. She was clearly struggling with her desire to embrace celibacy but shared with me that she experienced little if any encouragement from her support group, where a number of women saw genital involvement as quite compatible with their commitment to religious life. This surprised her, and we spent some time trying to understand the reasons for such a position.

It is my sense that her experience is not as exceptional as one might wish. Much of the confusion around celibacy originates, as I mentioned already, in the moral ambiguity of our time and in the general lack of purpose surrounding this vow. I do believe, however, that the years of silence and total disregard for psychosexual development in many of our congregations have rendered us especially vulnerable. Sexual orientation is not discovered, nor is the channeling of sexual energies learned, in a vacuum. If today much "discovery" or "experimentation" is going on even among older women and men religious who are normally expected to have worked through these issues, compassion and loving care are the appropriate responses, not scandal or rejection.

This is not to say that a total disregard for one's commitment can ever be the status quo. Sexual awakening is only part of the maturation story; it can never be our end. Whether it is comfortable for us to acknowledge this or not, however, we move into our commitment progressively and on ever-deepening levels of awareness. We do not take hold of it as much as it takes hold of us. For this, a journey into the art of relating and of loving is required, and, like all true art, this takes time and dedication.

Homosexuality

One of the greatest obstacles in this regard may be the fear among us, and in the Church generally, concerning diverse sexual orientations. Although there has been some movement toward greater acceptance and understanding, especially in some of our congregational literature,[59] the assumption that a homosexual orientation in religious life is the exception by far, and that it is debatable whether gay women or men should be accepted into religious life, nevertheless still seems to prevail. Not infrequently during seminars dealing with various topics concerning religious life, I find myself asked to address the question of homosexuality and the Church's position regarding sexual orientation. Some perceive the issue as a "growing problem," and I often spend considerable time assuring the questioner that homosexuality is new neither in the Church nor in religious life. It seems difficult for some to accept the fact that women and men with this orientation have always been part of our congregations as, indeed, they have been part of the human race. Due to the sexual repression many of them experienced, however, their inclinations may have remained vague for many of them. They also remained largely hidden from the rest of the congregation. The only difference today is that gay and lesbian religious are more aware of themselves and are able to express themselves more fully as sexual beings.

As most of us know, the official Church position on homosexuality accepts the "inclination" but condemns the act.[60] Much comment in the area of morality, Scripture study, and scientific investigation is available in response to this position.[61] The scope of our reflection, however, does not permit a digression into this valuable data. Suffice it here to take note of the almost universal plea among Catholic scholars for openness in this regard and for a willingness on the part of the magisterium to attend to scientific research in the areas of both scriptural interpretation and biology.

Perhaps one of the easiest as well as most readily accept-able discussions regarding the issue of sexual orientation is found in the article, "The Christian Body and Homosexual Maturity," by James R. Zullo and James D. Whitehead. The essay calls for the reconciliation with, and befriending of, our embodiment. The authors invite all of us, and homosexuals among us in par-ticular, toward "self-intimacy: listening to our own body, that it may tell us about ourself."[62] Along the road of self-intimacy, it becomes clear, they assure us, that "human sexuality will not be neatly divided between heterosexual and homosexual cat-egories." Rigid dichotomies here are misplaced: As I mature, "I realize that as a person I am not constituted in such a way as to be *exclusively* homosexual. Rather over a period of time,I ... more accurately come to know my sexual orien-tation as *predominantly* gay."[63] The same, it seems, holds true for heterosexuals, although the cultural assumptions around het-erosexuality as "only normal" make this process of coming to awareness less obvious. Orientation, therefore, is more correctly understood as existing on a continuum with predominant rather than exclusive characteristics.

Speaking for the maturing gay person in the process of self-acceptance, the authors observe:

> Within the realm of my predominant sexual orientation, I have experienced my affective life within a continuum which ranges from a whole constellation of homo-sexed responses on one end of the polarity to hetero-sexed re-sponses on the other. I have observed that my sexual orientation has not created barriers or blockades to the possibility of intimacy with persons of the opposite sex.

As a gay man, I realize that mutual self-disclosure, declarations of liking or loving, and demonstrations of affection can genuinely take place with women, and yet heterosexuality as a predominant sexual orientation is not my preferred mode of intimacy. Perhaps some of my confusion stems from the fact that many in our society tend to define sexual orientation in terms of genital behavior. For example, the fact that a lesbian may be quite capable of having sexual intercourse with a man and even enjoy it does not constitute her as a heterosexual woman. While it is true that consistent preferences for genital expression are key indicators for sexual orientation, what constitutes sexual orientation necessarily goes beyond the genital. More central to a definition of myself as gay or lesbian is the accumulated awareness I have of the movement of my affective life. Persistent patterns of homosexual attraction, enduring experiences of intimacy, and continuing manifestations of devoted love — these are the more trustworthy signs of my sexual orientation.[64]

The Expression of Intimacy

The tendency in our culture to put exclusive focus on genital activity and to identify sexual preference that way is not only thoroughly misleading, but also impoverishing. The experience of intimacy is so much richer than mere genital expression. It includes the deeper longing for relationship, affirmation, acceptance, loyalty, and trust. It allows for vulnerability and that other kind of nakedness that exposes the inner being and allows souls to meet. Thus, although expressing intimacy genitally is clearly an option, it need not necessarily be expressed that way, either for its own sake or for the discovery of one's primary orientation. Robert Nugent puts this somewhat starkly when he observes:

> The *homogenital* component of sexual orientation is more directly related to orgasmic pleasure, relief for sexual tensions, ecstasy, and pair-bonding. On the popular level the distinction is made between the one whom an individual "falls in love" with and the one with whom one "has sex." The former, especially for older people and over an extended period of time, is a more authentic indicator of sexual orientation than the latter.[65]

The distinction made here, once again, is of importance to both homosexuals and heterosexuals alike. It may also be of special interest to celibates. We renounce "having sex" but do not, by that fact, forego the possibility of "falling in love" and of learning much from that experience about ourselves and about human nature. Religious often mistakenly believe that by foregoing the genital expression of love, they renounce intimacy as well. This can have seriously debilitating effects on their growth into fully relational, alive, and loving persons.

It is clear that for the expression of intimacy, celibates will require great honesty both with themselves and the other. To begin with, there is no room here for "double-think," as Richard Sipe calls the "one or two lapses in the course of a year," that some do not consider "being sexually active," but see as merely relieving the stress caused by perpetual chastity.[66] What cannot be ignored or dismissed in any encounter is that human genital expression is directional and communicates personal commitment that an occasional "fling" belies. Genital *intimacy* is never merely coitus. Its humanness is constituted in its relationality; in its encounter with the other to whom one is answerable for the integrity of the message one communicates. The condoning of "sexual distractions" as normative "makes celibacy a farce and, more important, misses what Gandhi, for instance, knew so well — the tremendous power garnered from a life of *lived* celibacy."[67]

By the same token, celibate intimacy, as I have already pointed out, is learned. It is a disposition acquired, an art mastered over the years. Sipe acknowledges this when he calls it a *"process."* "Celibacy does not happen instantaneously," he points out. "It is the result of a history which progresses from an initial commitment to full celibate integration."[68] One's choice, therefore, not to express one's sexuality genitally but to embrace intimacy nevertheless, requires wisdom, realism, a certain "in-touchness," honesty, as well as great patience, especially with oneself. Contemplative awareness of one's own feelings, sensitivity toward the other, deep personal integrity, recognition of the message that is being communicated as well as of how it is being received, are all part of mature intimacy and of loving another honestly. They are not acquired overnight. Furthermore, the holistic spirituality within which we as celibates are called to operate invites us to stand in the polarities of our existence and to experience its tensions and its pain. It calls for a healthy realism that balances the clearly recognized forces of nature within with authentic care for creation and with the flow of energies in the universe calling for transformation and healing. Holistic spirituality and the celibacy it helps us live are never merely issues of intellectual assent or willpower. They affect every fiber of our being: the way we see ourselves and others; how we reach out to each other, live together; what we eat and drink; how we walk and talk, embrace and party, mourn and rejoice. If our celibacy is to be holy, we cannot deny our bodily ways of expressing love, fear, joy, pain. We need to connect ourselves with the ebb and flow of life; allow ourselves to feel it and to transmute it into healing power for the sake of the holy. This is not done easily or quickly.

The Need for Unlearning

The path of intimacy, in fact, is often an arduous and painful one, for it asks us not only to encounter and accept the otherness of the other, but also, and more importantly, to embrace ourselves. The latter is a prerequisite for the former even as, paradoxically, it is being brought about through it. Embracing oneself often asks for much unlearning, especially by those of us whose childhood needs for love were never adequately met. If we were among Alice Miller's "convenient" children,[69] who adjusted themselves to the poverty, violence, abuse, deprivation, overpopulation, or even death experiences in their homes by yielding to the needs of others rather than attending to their own, our adult relations will require much affective re-channeling, revisioning, and healing. This is never easy; it demands time, patience, and commitment.

Religious community life has not always been helpful here. The wounded person can be trying, and the others can be judgmental. Mistaken notions concerning "universal intimacy" among us often lead to bland niceness at best, and to the deadening of affect and general indifference at worst. When some openly reject the impossible and witness boldly to friendship, work at relationships, and struggle in the learning of intimacy, gossip and criticism, even in this day and age, can make their lives quite uncomfortable. I have discussed the childishness and harm of such persecution, as well as the serious damage it does to community life and to the sisterhood and brotherhood we profess, in *Living the Vision.*[70] Suffice it to say here that much work still needs to be done among us to help us toward a mature, holistic, and communal spirituality that accepts the growth needs of each member and empowers her or him toward full creativity. May's explanation of, and advice concerning, sexuality, spirituality, and creativity seems, in many respects, directly addressed to us:

In its fullest sense then, sexuality is nothing other than creative spirit: basic energy directed towards the enrichment and expansion of life. All endeavors that point toward greater depth and breadth of life can be said to be sexual. In this light spiritual searching, from its outset, could be called a sexual undertaking.

This leads us to a more refined understanding not only of how sexuality and spirituality are so intimately associated in the human psyche, but also of how their superficial manifestations can become mixed up and confused with each other. Further, it underscores the fact that a *thawing-out and integration of sexuality is a fundamental concomitant of spiritual growth.*

If people repress or stifle sexuality out of fear or guilt — *even in the guise of trying to be holy* — they will most likely also repress and stifle other expressions of creative living energy and wind up feeling and being only partially involved in the process of life. *This of course is not to say that spiritual growth requires genital expression.* As I have taken pains to point out, genital expression is a minor attribute that has little to do with the integration of full sexuality. Many very sexual, passionate, creative, spiritually mature people are celibate.[71]

Many, of course, are not, and many need not be, but *some are.* They have ruled out dualistic hatred of the body and do not experience fear of sexuality. They reject notions of "specialness" that give them an edge on ministry or place them in a "superior" vocation. They have accepted celibacy as a profoundly personal call and have responded to it out of a sense of what is uniquely required of *them.* Through this lifestyle they are moving into wholeness. Is it possible for us to gain a deeper understanding into the *how* of this, and to move toward personal appropriation?

Celibate Love

In his book on *Christian Zen*, William Johnston writes of the Oriental mystics' belief that "the celibate person (if he [she] is truly chaste) has increased spiritual power." In Oriental mysticism it is held that in lived celibacy sexual energy is converted to spiritual energy and results in strengthening one's quest for wisdom and in helping toward "the practice of contemplative love."[72] Johnston stresses the need for detachment as essential to mysticism. He doubts that "there is any detachment that cuts so deeply into the human fiber as celibacy. It creates an awful loneliness at the core of one's being, and it is precisely from this emptiness that the blind stirring of love takes its origin."[73] The similarity between Johnston's perspective and Gerald May's reflections on root spiritual energy as the dynamic source of love is clear (Part II, "The Transmutation of Energy"). How the celibate can understand her or his life as a practice of contemplative love, however, will need some further reflection.

Gerald May posits three manifestations of root spiritual energy or "agapic love," as he calls it. He understands these as processed and differentiated expressions of love that, through the human psyche and in varying degrees, give witness to it:

> It is as if agape were the base metal, irreducible and
> unadulterated. It can be experienced in part, but it can-
> not be comprehended or analyzed. Bits of it, however,
> can be taken into the psyche as fragments of energy,
> alloyed with certain aspects of self-definition, and thus
> appear in conscious human experience as *narcissism,*
> *erotic* or *filial* love, or as some other emotion.[74]

The fundamental human longing for "a love that is given
and granted without reservation"; that "is contingent on no performance, no attribute, no personal whim or desire," takes form
through these three expressions of love.[75] It remains ultimately
unfulfilled, however, since it craves the totality of love — the
love "that has the power to truly cast out fear," and no human
fragmented expression can satisfy it.

Narcissistic Love

The narcissistic love of early childhood frequently sets the stage
for the drama of longing that we experience as we mature. The
healthy sense of well-being, of belonging, of being safe and embraced in the unconditional love of our mother or significant
other is rarely realized. Narcissistic disorder is not uncommon,
therefore, and religious are no exception here. Much of the "unlearning" mentioned previously in connection with expressions
of intimacy is connected with the expectations spawned by childhood deprivation, and releasement here is painful.

Even more severe and often detrimental to growth in love is
adult narcissism. It is characterized by excessive self-absorp-

tion — an inordinate need to receive rather than give, a utilization of others for one's own interests. Some hold that self-preservation is the biological root of narcissism; selfishness can easily be its result. The world is seen as revolving around us; our own personal pleasure and well-being become the focal point of all our decisions. There is here a fixation — a stagnation, if you will — of the love energy that longs for expression in us. The need for personal affirmation and acceptance, for "specialness" and recognition, overwhelms us. We, in fact, misconstrue cravings for needs and become addicts to our own longing. We cannot understand why others will not supply us with what we "should" have. Erich Fromm gives an interesting example of this, which, in its ordinariness, gives pause for thought:

> A man calls the doctor's office and wants an appointment. The doctor says that he cannot make an appointment for that same week, and suggests a date for the following. The patient insists on his request for an early appointment, and as an explanation does not say, as one might expect, why there is such urgency, but mentions the fact that he lives only five minutes away from the doctor's office. When the doctor answers that his own time problem is not solved by the fact that it takes so little time for the patient to come to his office, the latter shows no understanding; he continues to insist that he has given a good enough reason for the doctor to give him an early appointment.[76]

One can smile at this and shake one's head. What is of interest to us, however, is the inability of this individual to *see* another's situation as something separate from his own. All this man *can* see is his own perspective.

Although the extreme blindness here may be infrequent in our day-to-day experience, narcissism as such is not. We can even be quite religious and maintain that our concern is for God's will, while in reality we are obsessing about ourselves. Obsessive guilt — the preoccupation with what *I* have done, with *my* conscience, *my* reputation, the scandal or "disedification" *I* have caused, what others will say about *me* — is a form of narcissism. *Moral hypochondriasis* is what Fromm calls it.[77] It expresses self-absorption negatively and is characterized by feelings of inadequacy and self-accusation.

As a narcissist, I have no sense of the other's otherness. Different from healthy self-regard and its appreciation for covenantal relationship and responsibility, narcissism in religious life isolates me. I live apart, even as I expect everyone's concern to coincide with mine. *My* ministry, *my* sabbatical, *my* "charge," *my* room, *my* privacy, *my* favorite television program, all become focal points in *my* world. And *my* world is *the* world. I understand community in terms of it and cannot comprehend how anyone could possibly have views different from mine — desire to recreate differently, or not share my tastes. I see ministry (or the lack thereof) in terms of *my* agenda as well. Since my world is *the* world, I expect everyone to understand and appreciate why I do what I do: When I work, no one can possibly work as hard and be as good; when I refuse to work, the community will, of course, take care of my every need, and anyone who dares to challenge my perpetual sabbatical is simply unjust and does not understand religious life.

In interpersonal relationships, my dismissal of anyone who

does not respond to my expectations of friendship reciprocally as "not being in touch," as "being unkind," even "cruel"; my inability to see that another does not have to feel in kind ("it is impossible that she or he does not love me when I love her or him so much") are also forms of narcissism.[78] Any rejection of criticism or challenge to me as simply "not understanding me," holds the self as central and normative. May sees adult narcissism as "the single most difficult *obstacle* to more mature forms of loving."[79] It is clearly the least developed, and fixation here poses major difficulties for community life.

Erotic Love

Erotic love might be seen as the symbol *par excellence* of creativity. It is the love of genital intimacy, although it is so much more than mere genitality. "The interpersonal fusion of eroticism, like nuclear fusion, can liberate extremes of creative or destructive energy."[80] It is the subject of poetry and song and is portrayed in theater, films, novels, and even advertising. Wars have been fought over it and lives freely sacrificed. It is the single most popular topic for conversation. Our culture is obsessed with it. It vitalizes, activates, drives. In its throes one seems inexhaustible. It is the "wonder-filled and dramatic attachment of one person to another that results in such global preoccupation that a 'fusion' occurs in which the external world simply 'falls away.'"[81]

Although celibates abstain from the genital expression of erotic love, its experience in their day-to-day lives is not thereby denied. Often the beginning phases of friendship carry much of its energy: There is need of the other's presence. There is a hunger for privacy, for sharing, for mutual attention, for affection. "Wonder-filled and dramatic attachments" are not foreign to religious. Foregoing the genital expression of love does not exempt us from the natural ways love emerges in human encounters. Falling in love is precisely that: It "befalls us" very much beyond our control or planning. This can happen to religious just as easily as it happens to other persons.

Love slays. It calls for surrender and creativity. Always it has much to teach us about ourselves, if we but let ourselves learn. Love brings pain, anguish, ecstasy. What we do with the experience for the sake of preserving the intimacy it calls for as well as of standing by the commitment we have made is, of course, open to adult decisions. This does not mean, however, that it is easy and can be handled without risk. Nevertheless, I cannot help wishing the experience on everyone, for there is nothing quite like erotic love to get us in touch with our vulnerability as well as our power; to help us appreciate, therefore, the human condition.

Filial Love

The third manifestation of root spiritual energy, filial love, speaks to what we have discussed already as the ascetical/apostolic motivation for our celibate lifestyle. May describes it as

> [a] firm, committed, noncontrived giving of time, energy, attention, and wealth to further the welfare and improve the lives of other human beings. It is the 'brotherly [sisterly] love' of Christianity. It is also parental love. Filial love is characterized not only by concern for the plight of other people but also by identifying and empathizing with their condition.[82]

It arises out of the experience of compassion that stands with the other in her or his suffering and struggle and recognizes something of me there. It sees life energy as shared and accepts participation as well as mutuality in the quest for a better life. It puts its life on the line for others.

The love energy of the universe is, in filial love, channeled not primarily toward the beloved other to whom I may be drawn through erotic attachment, but rather to the at times unlovable, to the hurting, to those in need. If filial love is identified as one's major motivation for celibacy, there is, in the mature understanding of this, no rejection of genital love as a valuable expression of creative energy. The celibate may simply recognize that genital expressions of love are abundant and hold great attraction. They are dear to the human heart. In many cultures, and especially in ours, they are also often overused or abused and misrepresented. Celibates, no doubt, are drawn to the magnetism and beauty of genital love but feel that channeling creative energy into its other and often its more neglected and less understood expressions needs their exclusive attention. This then becomes the motivation for their life's choice. Most of us know that the charism of our congregation finds its reason here. It, in no way, was or is a rejection of the other expressions of love. It merely channels love where it is seen to be in greater need of manifestation, where it needs to be proclaimed.

It seems that the vow of poverty, as I have reflected on it in *Living the Vision*, is particularly oriented to this kind of love and is, therefore, a valuable support to celibacy. It speaks of solidarity with the oppressed and sees all works on behalf of justice and mercy as "guided and supported by a fundamental disposition of uncompromising at-oneness with the human family"[83]:

Holistic spirituality is the journey toward a soft heart. When I experience in the very core of my being those who bleed as shedding my blood; those who hunger as aching with my pain; those who sin as performing my deeds; when I truly encounter the gift that is the human community even in its darkest moments and, deeper still, know myself to hold that darkness as well, then I am at one with humankind groaning for the fullness of creation, the fullness of our redemption in Christ.[84]

This is, I believe, the depth insight of filial love. This is the energy out of which it flows. It holds incredible power and motivation. For its sake many have spent their lives; many also have died. It is the stuff that martyrs are made of: Gandhi, Romero, the six Jesuits and four women martyrs of El Salvador; the martyrs of Liberia, and women and men all over the world whose love stands primarily, sometimes exclusively, with the poor and disenfranchised against oppression, in spite of violence and in the face of death.

Celibate Love

It seems from our reflection thus far that the three manifestations of root spiritual energy, as Gerald May discusses them, are all somehow available for experience in the life of religious. Any one can become primary for us and motivate our behavior for better or worse. All are present to some degree. The call to celibacy seems motivated, however, largely by filial love, and one can find deep fulfillment there.

What then, we still need to ask ourselves, are we to make of the "blind stirring of love" that William Johnston sees as originating at the core of our celibate emptiness? What of the "something more" toward which the celibate choice is said to be directed not for any *other* reason than *longing itself* — a hunger, an emptiness felt? Where might we find it; how might we experience it? Where does it fit?

May reflects on "agapic love." He says it transcends us, it is not influenced by our desires or our whims, is not deserved or removed. It alone "casts out fear," is unconditional, eternal.[85] Agapic love cannot be earned, is ever present but frequently unnoticed. It is the ground of our loving as well as love itself. Love, we are told, lures us, and yet nothing in our power can access it. It is pure gift longing to bestow itself, the energy that sustains the universe present deep in our hearts. John of the Cross, it seems, experienced it. He refers to it as the

> Living flame of love
> That tenderly wounds my soul
> In its deepest center![86]

Mechtild of Magdeburg knew it also, as "the rippling tide of love [that] flows secretly out from God into the soul and draws it mightily back to its Source."[87] She speaks of fire, of the "underground river," of the "flowing Godhead," of compassion. Julian of Norwich, in turn, wants us to understand it as "motherhood"; Hildegard of Bingen as "warm moistness," as "greening power."

Scientists today speak of it also, with awe: Adolf Portmann calls it a "non-spatial abyss of mystery," a "primal ground." Walter Heitler sees a "spiritual principle." Lincoln Barnett writes of a "featureless unity of space–time, mass–energy, matter–field

— an ultimate, undiversified, and eternal ground."[88] David Bohm invites us to ponder the "superimplicate order that lies beyond the domain of time."[89] All approach it, acknowledge it. None can fathom it. The mystics are touched by it; science is mystified in the face of it. Gerald May perhaps speaks for most when he observes: "I cannot presume to know the biological or metaphysical 'purpose' behind agape. But it does impart an unquestionable sense of meaning to existence whenever it is realized. Certainly its realization satisfies human spiritual longing; *it brings us home.*"[90]

There is a universality here that transcends traditional religious language. "Breath" or "light" symbolize agape's presence perhaps most closely: "If breath symbolizes that which permits life to exist in the first place, then light symbolizes that which allows us to perceive the wonder of living."[91] Above all, however, it is known as gift, and *we believe it is God.* "God is love, and those who abide in love abide in God, and God abides in them" (1 John 4:16).

I would like to think that somehow our celibate commitment can be recognized as pointing toward this love and as accepting emptiness as its symbolic witness. I would like to understand celibacy as lifelong expectancy or readiness, as a hollowness waiting, as one way humans acknowledge their vulnerability and dependency in a world that seems so self-sufficient, as "a voice crying in the wilderness" that Love is and that Love fulfills.

So often in our traditions the religious quest is seen anthropologically, as initiated somehow by *us* in response to *our* yearning. We seek meaning; we search for God; we hunger for love and reach out in love. The ascetical/apostolic motivation for celibacy, within the context of filial love, surely finds its interpretation there: God calls, and we respond to the needs of our time through service and the choice of this lifestyle as, for us, the most suitable. We experience our vocation as a love-response to God in Christ. What if, however, we were to switch the focus? What if the anthropological would yield to the cosmic, and we would understand the call to celibacy as *God's* yearning, as *God's* breaking out in us, as *God's* "unfolding in us and through us" and moving us toward surrender to the divine embrace?

Willigis Jäger, in his recently translated book, *Searching for the Meaning of Life*, explains what I am trying to explore by suggesting, in fact, that "the Divine comes to consciousness in us."

> We think that as human beings we are on a quest for God. But we're not the ones searching for Ultimate Reality. Rather it is the Ultimate Reality that causes the dissatisfied yearning and the search in us. God is the seeker. God awakens in us. We ourselves can't *do* anything; we can only let go so the Divine can unfold itself. We can only "get out of God's way," as Eckhart says. The essential nature reveals itself if only we don't prevent it. And if there is a redemption, then we are redeemed from being possessed by our ego so that our real selves can spread their wings.[92]

Perhaps our celibate emptiness emerges as a form of ego-surrender; as a conscious focusing on the primacy of the divine; as a sign that points beyond human choice and even beyond good works to cosmic yearning, to the "groaning" that Paul writes about (Romans 8: 22). Perhaps celibacy can be seen as giving ourselves over to the no-thingness that underlies all things, as a making available of space for no-thing in particular — space, rather, for the *all* in all. Perhaps celibacy *needs* to be pointless so that it can be the gathering place for the Light — disturbed by no refractions or reflections — because of emptiness. Perhaps celibacy symbolizes the "yes" spoken in the depth of one's being — over the span of a lifetime, to God's incarnation. As such its physical renunciation is merely a pointer toward a cosmic event that surpasses all human initiative and is meant for all.

Henri Nouwen sees celibacy as a *Vacare Deo*, a being empty and, as such, a witnessing to the one who "is the quiet center of all human life."[93] The celibate, he says, is "a visible witness for the inner sanctum in *all* people's lives." Within this context,

> it becomes clear that sexual abstinence can never be the most important aspect of celibacy. Not being married or not being involved in a sexual relationship does not constitute the celibate life. Celibacy is an openness to God of which sexual abstinence is only one of its manifestations. *Celibacy is a life-style in which we try to witness to the priority of God in all relationships.*[94]

The celibate vocation radically witnesses to the primacy of agapic love, to the grounding of all human longing in God's yearning for us. I believe that our life is "compelled" into celibacy by the fundamental recognition of all of creation's radical orientation toward God, in whom alone love can find its fulfillment. Our call is to bear in our bodies the realization, so poignantly expressed by Karl Rahner, that

> everything else exists so that this one thing might be: the eternal miracle of infinite Love. And so God makes a creature whom [God] can love: [God] creates [human-kind]. [God] creates [us] in such a way that we *can* receive this love which is God himself [herself], and that [we] can and must at the same time accept it for what it is: the ever astounding wonder, the unexpected, unexacted gift.[95]

Mature celibacy lives in this wonder and aches with this love. God's is a longing and a loving "so intense" that indeed it "terrifies." It is enticement, however, as well — the sweet lure that costs "not less than everything" (T.S. Eliot). The "love of God impels us." It graces us at the same time. Bearing witness to this is a vocation worth the pain. Our recognition of this, however, is not easily won. Many of us do so only retroactively, as it were, after years of living it. The "seven years" in our forest dwelling can stretch over a lifetime, therefore, and we often find ourselves wandering aimlessly in the wilderness for a long, long time. Celibacy is perhaps best understood as an event whose sacredness gives itself to us mostly in glimpses and unfolds only very slowly. Its vision, however, when it graces us, opens us ultimately to serenity and peace. It gives us freedom.

Questions for Focus, Reflection, and Discussion

1. "The more of myself that I forget, deny, repress and suppress in one relationship, the more partial, the more limited, the more impoverished will be the relationship." Is this statement relevant to us and to the Church, with respect to the neglected feminine dimension in our midst? What might "coming home to ourselves" mean in this regard?

2. What are the "silver-handed" standards or values that our congregations treasure? Have they thwarted creativity among us?

3. Are we partially responsible for the denial of the feminine in our midst, for silencing its voice and denying its vision? If so, how is this different in men's communities than in women's?

4. What does it mean for us to "live by the rules of the king's garden"? Have some of us reached "the zero point, where life is reduced to absolutely nothing, and everything opens up to radical doubt"? If so, what does this mean for us, for our commitment to our congregations, our way of life?

5. Is it true that "only if it hurts enough will we change"? If not, what are the radical changes we are willing to embrace for the sake of life and wholeness?

6. What is the relationship in our congregations between leadership and administration? Do we expect too much from those we elect? Are we abdicating personal responsibility

and indulging in unwarranted dependency? Do we allow ourselves to be "warehoused" — taken care of without assuming our part of the covenant?

7. What does it mean to be a forest dweller — individually, congregationally? How does it bring about a soft heart? Do we at times "process" ourselves away from or out of the forest in which so many of us are called to dwell? If so, what specific behaviors indicate that we do? Why do we?

8. Do you agree that celibacy seems to remain the least discussed and most "unreflected" of the vows? Why do we vow celibacy?

9. "Unless issues of psychosexual development are dealt with, morality cannot be addressed meaningfully. Its precepts may be known, but it oppresses and debilitates rather than guides human behavior." What is your reaction to this observation? How might this apply to celibacy?

10. In "Why Celibacy Today?" a variety of reasons are given for this vow. Do you relate to any of them?

11. How can the celibate bear witness "to the primacy of all of humanity's initial as well as final God-directedness"? It is clear that for this to happen, abstinence alone is not enough. What is it that is required?

12. Has the reflection on the "transmutation of energy" as discussed by Gerald May been helpful to you? If so, how? If not, why not?

13. How have you come to understand Frankl's "paradoxical intention" and May's nonattachment? How could either of them help in moving us away from excessive control toward healthy living?

14. Is it possible to experience intimacy without a genital

encounter, passion without its erotic expression? How do you see the distinction Nugent makes between "falling in love" or "being in love" and "having sex"?

15. What was your reaction to the reflections on homosexuality in religious life? What does it mean to be "reconciled with," and to "befriend" one's embodiment, to listen to our own bodies so that they may tell us about ourselves?

16. What are we to understand by the observation that sexual "orientation is more correctly understood as a continuum with predominant rather than exclusive characteristics"?

17. What are we to understand by celibacy as a process into which I commit myself and into which I move over the years — celibate intimacy as having to be learned? Is this process of learning different from, or does it include, what Sipe's calls "one or two lapses during the course of a year" to relieve tension? What is celibate "double-think"?

18. What is your reaction to the observation that "much work still needs to be done among us to help us toward a mature, holistic, and communal spirituality that accepts the growth needs of each member and empowers her or him toward full creativity"?

19. How relevant to religious life is the discussion in "Celibate Love" on narcissism, on erotic love, on filial love?

20. "I would like to understand celibacy as lifelong expectancy or readiness; as a hollowness waiting, as one way humans acknowledge their vulnerability and dependency in a world that seems so self-sufficient, as 'a voice crying in the wilderness' that Love *is* and that Love fulfills." After having reflected on agapic love as described in "Celibate Love," what is your reaction to this observation?

III

On Welcoming the New

Situating Ourselves

In 1989, with visionary courage, the Leadership Conference of Women Religious and the Conference of Major Superiors of Men in joined assembly dared to dream. They came together, looked at what they were, and then leaped ahead some twenty years, dreaming of who they could be. They shared their vision with us in a small document entitled "Future of Religious Life," listing ten transfomative elements that would bring this future about.

The element that I found of particular interest, and to which I already devoted some reflections in *Where Two or Three Are Gathered*, is the leadership's dream for inclusivity and intentionality in community, element 8:

> In 2010 we will be characterized by inclusivity and intentionality. Our communities may include persons of different ages, genders, cultures, races, and sexual orientation. They may include persons who are lay or cleric, married or single, as well as vowed and/or unvowed members. They will have a core group and persons with temporary and permanent commitments.

Our communities will be ecumenical, possibly interfaith; faith-sharing will be constitutive of the quality
of life in this context of expanded membership. Such
inclusivity will necessitate a new understanding of membership and a language to accompany it.

Religious life still includes religious congregations
of permanently vowed members.

Not everyone with whom I have discussed this vision cares
for it. One sister from Europe who had read my discussion of it
in *Where Two or Three Are Gathered* wanted to know what would
in fact distinguish religious congregations from any ordinary
village if this element became a reality. An interesting point! In
citing the document in my book, I had omitted its reference to
"a core group and persons with temporary and permanent commitment." This might have reassured her. I had, however, not
been prepared, nor had I intended to reassure. There was and is
no doubt in my mind that the vision of 1989 was far-ranging
and radical and, therefore, disturbing. In raising it here, I once
again do not wish to talk us out of the discomfort it might in-
spire. I would rather ask us where we are some seven years
after it was written.

Perhaps no one knows as well as we do how good we can be
at strategizing and planning, at writing objectives and mission
statements. We can, however, also all too easily fall prey to
what I have come to call the "Cartesian affliction": We can
come to delude ourselves that when we write, it *is* — it happens. Unfortunately, this is not the way things work. If what
the transformative elements project as a future for us is to come
about, if all our subsequent outlined steps for new models of

membership are to become a reality for us, then our statements have to carry with them commitment. They have to carry the weight of covenant. They have to become soul pledges, linking our faithfulness to the abiding faithfulness of God. Is this what is happening for us today? Have our congregations caught the fire that inspired the 1989 vision? Is it being implemented, or has it remained on the pages on which it was written — one more document for our files? It is clear that those who wrote it cannot bring it about by themselves. It is my hope, however, that when they wrote it they spoke the communal vision, the congregational dream; that they sensed where we were heading and opened to the Spirit that was driving us. Did they?

There can be great disease when one stands as delegate for one's congregation. It is indeed a humbling experience that calls for profound discernment regarding the will of God in the *now* as well as for the *not yet.* I can remember clearly feeling a deep apprehension when, as a delegate to one of the General Chapters in my own community, I realized how much we were being carried away by the experience and vision of the moment as we were all writing directives for the congregation's next six years. Our vision came in many respects from what *we* had witnessed in the here-and-now, what *we* had heard, what *we* had experienced, what *we* had shared. It was inspired no doubt by the urgency *we* felt and that was, of course, what one would expect. My dis-ease did not originate, therefore, in our experience as such, but rather in the recognition that the other twenty-four hundred or so Sisters of Notre Dame who were not there needed somehow to catch the same vision, feel the same energy, if our Chapter acts were going to amount to anything at all beyond the printed page. And here pious platitudes about "being their delegate" or "speaking on their behalf" simply won't wash any more. Congregational documents, as we all know, have a quiet way of slipping into the bottom of drawers or hiding on top shelves where they gather dust along with indifference until another set is placed on top of them. We all know that the days of decreed vision are over — if, indeed, they ever existed. The time has come to match dreams with the truth of who we are, and this demands radical honesty.

It is clear that the issue raised by transformative element 8 revolves around our opening up and widening our horizons. It is also clear that some aspects of its agenda are easier to achieve than others. Some may, in fact, be already present and need only to be realized and celebrated. A case in point is diversity in sexual orientation. Our discussion in Part II of this book may perhaps make it easier for us at this point to acknowledge our reality in this regard, to understand it more fully, and to grow more at ease with it. The associate programs in many congregations also manifest movement toward inclusivity. Their objective is the welcome of men and women, married and single, un-vowed persons and even clergy. It would appear, at first glance, therefore, that we are making headway in our response to element 8. It is true that cultural and racial diversity does not seem to have improved in the congregations of what is broadly referred to as the "Western world," but here we can, of course, cite the general decline of our membership as a credible excuse. The possibility of ecumenical and even interfaith communities is also still unrealized and, at best, a radical exception. Once again, however, we can explain this by citing our canonical status as an excuse. What remains to be looked at, then, regarding element 8, after all is said and done and all our explanations given, is an ever-decreasing number of aging, vowed members.

And even as I write this, I ask myself the uneasy question: What is really changing? Is this all we can say here? And if so, where is the new energy in all of this, the welcome of the different? Have we in fact *tangibly* changed our world to accommodate diversity, or did we simply appoint someone to coordinate peripheral things while the rest of us keep on keeping on? Why is it that, although in many congregations the number of associates seems to be growing and is at times larger by far than the vowed membership in various units, we nevertheless keep worrying about diminishment, about our founder's charism, about extinction? Why is it *really* that in a country of such ethnic diversity as the United States, women and men of different cultures and races are almost completely absent in our midst?

What's Wrong with
This Picture?

I belong to a support group made up of women from six different congregations in the area. Of late we have taken to playing
our own version of the well-known childhood game, "What's
Wrong with This Picture?" A growing associate membership,
even as vowed membership worries about safeguarding the
charism and about their own diminishment, would be a "picture" for our consideration. At issue, it seems, is the term "membership," and the question is clearly: "What do we really mean
by it?"

   Are vowed members the only guardians of the charism —
the ones solely responsible, who care for it, protect it, teach it?
Can we alone carry out the intention of our respective congregations and bring their founding inspiration to fulfillment? Is
vowed membership an absolute requirement for full status in a
congregation? The immediate and obvious answer for many of
us seems to be a "yes," and yet I wonder if for the sake of life
and the future of our founding charism we could not allow ourselves to consider different options. I know of a congregation
whose numbers are so small that for the sake of their charism

they have taken to living with, as well as working with, lay persons both married and single who, they hope, will carry on the mission and witness to the charism long after all the vowed members have gone or are too old to minister. The vowed members of this community are facing their reality honestly and courageously, and they are the happier and more creative for it. But truth such as they have to face is difficult to endure. Those of us who are larger in number but nonetheless aging rapidly can more easily ignore it for yet some time. We can talk of "vocation directors" and "younger members." We can resist more mature applicants, look for interested persons in colleges and even high schools and deny our misplaced expectations. (A friend of mine calls it "cruel and unusual punishment" to expect any twenty-year-old to live forever with her grandmothers.) We can ask the most energetic and the brightest among us to give up valuable and important ministries for the Church so that they can spend their time attracting new members, "bringing them in," and "forming" the one or two who actually do come. And all the while we seem merely to be rewriting an old script — "renovating the old in a new shell," "rebuilding or regilding" it, as Joan Chittister would say,[1] and ignoring our reality.

A vignette is told by Allan Sager in his book, *Gospel-Centered Spirituality: An Introduction to Our Spiritual Journey,* that speaks, I believe, to us these days:

> I could hardly believe my eyes when I saw the
> name of the shop: THE TRUTH SHOP.
> It was just where I wanted to be.
> The saleswoman was very polite: "What type of
> truth do you wish to purchase," she asked,

"partial or whole?"

"Why, the whole truth, of course." No deception
for me, no rationalizations. I wanted my truth
plain and unadulterated.
She waved me on to another side of the store.
The saleswoman there pointed to the price tag.
"The price is very high, sir," she warned.
"What is it?" I asked, determined to get the whole
truth, no matter what it cost.
"Your security, sir," she answered.[2]

The vignette ends with the man leaving. He could not afford that price. How do we relate to this story? What truth
presents itself to us about our life in contemporary times, and
can we face it? Are we willing to "buy" it? Can we, without
negating the vowed life but also without closing the door to other
ways of carrying on the congregation's mission, accept the reality that offers itself to us in our times, the truth that invites us to
rethink and revision our options?

It seems, as Patricia Wittberg indicates, that the associational
model of membership is now the predominant model for many
congregations. "As many as fifty to sixty percent of the active
religious in some of these congregations," she estimates,
"are living singly or in pairs, and come together with a larger
group of their fellow members only periodically for prayer or
discussion meetings."[3] Unlike in the past when unity demanded
proximity and often uniformity in ministry, these religious are
scattered throughout the country and sometimes even abroad.

It is clear that this phenomenon has radically altered the
way community life is viewed, the way we connect and bond

with one another, and the way we find and give support. Whether this situation has been chosen — has been decided upon and implemented by the congregation as a whole — is not always clear. What *is* clear, however, is that it has become our reality or at least the reality for many of us. Whereas this may be seen as unfortunate by some, it is considered their salvation by others and may, in some cases, be the only way they see themselves staying in religious life. The notion of "holding all things in common" has, therefore, taken on a different perspective. Simplicity of lifestyle and sharing are still very much part of religious life, but they look different now. So does obedience and the responsibility it now demands. Corporate ministries have for many of us been rethought and reevaluated. There is a separateness now in our togetherness that was unthinkable when we all lived in convents and shared the same horarium, meals, and petty cash. We often live far apart from one another, closer to other congregations. Our support systems are, therefore, widespread and inclusive of non-religious, of women and men, married and single.

What does all of this tell us about ourselves? Is what has happened and continues to happen unfortunate? Should we feel regret? Should we retrench, undo, reformulate? Can we? Or ought we ask ourselves instead whether it is really necessary to see what we are experiencing today negatively? If so, what are the reasons for our negativity? Could they lie, perhaps, in our fear of the radically different? Might we be resistant simply because things are not what they used to be; because they are different from what worked for us when we were young, from what seemed so holy and so right then? What would happen, on the other hand, if we would allow ourselves to see that our present reality, in fact, is telling us something new about our congregational mandate, about how the charism can be and is being spread, and how our founding inspiration is taking on new forms and is blossoming? Why must this phenomenon necessarily be the sign of "creeping individualism"? Might it not be that the women and men, spread all over the country and the globe, are burning with the same flame that the small band of founders felt; that the love of Christ, indeed, is impelling them (Paul, 2 Corinthians 5:14); that they are feeling something in their bones that is good and wholesome, something that speaks of the reign and invites our consideration? Could it not perhaps be that, in the radical insecurity that our very diversity seems to hold in store, the new is beckoning? And could not the new invite us to the very inclusivity that we seem so afraid of and often organize ourselves away from even as we profess it? Might it be, as one of my friends suggested to me not long ago, that *relationality* is emerging as a new charism for religious life in the post-modern era?

And the Young Shall
See Visions, the Old Shall
Dream Dreams

W hat if we accepted the associational model as part of who we are — not as an idiosyncrasy, an anomaly that is but temporary and will go away when all the sisters and brothers "come home" again and start living, once more, in community houses? What if we accepted a mixture of Wittberg's models for our present reality, and reconciled ourselves to the fact that mixtures tend to be messy but may be more real? What if we let go of any model as *the* model: saw intentional communities, as Wittberg describes them,[4] as helpful for some of us; bureaucratic aspects as enhancing efficiency wherever that is needed (especially in large congregations, where personnel departments, administrative job descriptions, grievance procedures, and so on, make for clarity in leadership); allowed for the associational model as a contemporary reality that opens up the possibility of new forms of membership?

Without suggesting the "what if's" I have presented above as ideal, and being fully aware of the mind shift that would be required, I could nevertheless envision some interesting possibilities for our future. For one, it seems to me that we could find ourselves broadening our membership base considerably, and that we could do this without having to abandon our covenantal commitment, or our resolve to share our resources. Women and men could join religious communities without necessarily having to leave their homes, apartments, and even relational ties. Since living in common is an option but not a requirement for membership, those not doing so but imbued, nevertheless, with the vision of the respective congregation and committed to its corporate vision (as many of our associates already are) could in fact be free to apply for full membership, to share their resources and share ours, and to become actively involved with the congregation. There could be a wide range of membership possibilities. The new members might take some of the traditional vows, if their life permits. They could add others within the context of the congregational charism, such as "hospitality," "mercy," or "service." We would, of course, keep living the vows we love — not because they make us better and present a superior lifestyle, but because we see them as our way of living our baptismal consecration, and because we feel called to them.

The primary objective in all of this would be to broaden the mission base and to allow for new life — new forms of life and possibly even the return of former members in new ways as well. A conversation I had with a regional superior of the Sisters of Mercy in Australia recently brought this last point home to me with particular sensitivity. She told me of one of their former members who was on staff in one of their large "Mater" Hospitals. One night while she was working the evening shift in the admissions area, a street person came in and sat down in the waiting area. He told her simply that he needed shelter, and that what was printed on the plaque in the foyer told him he could get it here. At a loss as to what to do with him, she let him sit there during her shift, but as it became time for her to leave she found herself in a quandary as to how to proceed: "I finally asked myself, 'What would Catherine have done?'" she said, "and then I simply decided to put him up for the night." The sister who shared this story with me wondered why women such as these could not be part once again of our congregations. Was not, in this case, the spirit of Mercy plainly evident? What is it that has made so many of our former members leave? Would not a broader and more inclusive membership model allow them to be where they truly belong?

Such a model would undoubtedly facilitate the founding inspiration of the congregation in numerous ways. This does not necessarily mean that its objective would be limited merely to continuing the congregation's "works" per se — that is, to keep its institutions open. Many of these were not present in the founding years of the community and are merely expressions of its response to the needs of a particular time in its history. Facilitating the founding inspiration in our day means above all seeking out, as our early founders did, the most neglected and the abandoned of our time and standing with them in whatever way we can; being their voice and, better yet, helping them gain their own voice. In amazingly creative ways the traditional call to teach, to heal, to proclaim God's goodness, to witness to mercy or charity can take on new modes of expression in our time. For this we need life and energy. And this is where we must be.

With respect to permanent or temporary commitment, the new model could offer the option for either. Temporary commitments would be renewable and could open up the chance that even the one-year commitment of a mission volunteer be extended into more involved membership as time went on and experience deepened. Involvement in the congregation's internal workings would depend on one's commitment. It would not, however, be seen hierarchically — some commitments being viewed as better or higher than others. The primary criteria would be relevance and practicality instead. For example, a member who does not share resources does not vote on them. Someone who does not permanently commit herself or himself to the congregation does not decide the retirement policy.

Hierarchism is, of course, one of the major obstacles to even considering a broadened base of active membership. It is the "deep-down elitism" I referred to in Part I ("On Regrounding Our Values") that has us put status over value. There is no doubt that a broadened base for membership will not happen if some of us will persist in seeing ourselves or our way of living out our charism as better than any other's. Only the leveling vision of Elisabeth Schüssler Fiorenza's "society of equals" will bring this about. But it is entirely possible that some of us, even with the holiest of intentions, will not get it and will prefer to let the charism die, smothered in pious platitudes instead.

> In the ministry of Jesus God is experienced as all-inclusive love. ... This God is a God of graciousness and goodness who accepts everyone and brings about justice and well-being for everyone without exception. The creator God accepts all members of Israel ... as long as they are prepared to engage in the perspective and power of the *basileia*. ... Sophia, the God of Jesus, wills the wholeness and humanity of everyone and therefore en-

ables the Jesus movement to become a "discipleship of equals." They are called to one and the same praxis of inclusiveness and equality lived by Jesus-Sophia.[5]

It is here, I believe, in the living out of this ideal to the best of our ability and in prophetic witness to what Christianity is all about, that the religious community of tomorrow will identify its difference from "any ordinary village." I rather doubt that our purpose has ever been to establish ourselves as "different from," in the strict sense of "separation" implied here. Is our life not significant, rather, because of our being, or at least try-ing to be, "one with"? Is that not what the title of "Sister" or "Brother" implied, and is it not legitimate to wonder why in so many cases it has lost the symbol of solidarity and has become a sign of distinction instead?

Identifying for ourselves what inclusivity will look like, and how authentic relating in the midst of all this diversity will hap-pen, will not be an easy task. In the last analysis, however, it will most likely not be a "task" at all but will instead emerge out of an attitude that is already being lived by many of us and needs only to be recognized, ratified, and accepted by the whole. That the process of emergence will present major difficulties and may be met with great resistance cannot be denied. The fear of cri-tiquing and possibly relinquishing long-cherished priorities can not be underestimated. It can paralyze us for years to come. So also can canon law and "who" it tells us we may or may not count among us. The moment has, however, already come, and the inclusion is already happening — quietly, among those who live too far away to experience intimacy with their own congre-gational membership; among those who work outside, in the diaspora regions of the congregation; among those who have reached out and have recognized the wholesomeness and beauty of it all.

In the Meantime

Nikos Kazantzakis tells this story:

I remember one morning when I discovered a cocoon in the bark of a tree, just as the butterfly was making a hole in its case and preparing to come out. I waited a while, but it was too long appearing and I was impatient. I bent over it and breathed on it to warm it. I warmed it as quickly as I could and the miracle began to happen before my eyes, faster than life. The case opened, the butterfly started slowly crawling out and I shall never forget my horror when I saw how its wings were folded back and crumpled; the wretched butterfly tried with its whole trembling body to unfold them. Bending over it, I tried to help it with my breath. In vain. It needed to be hatched out patiently and the unfolding of the wings should be a gradual process in the sun. Now it was too late. My breath had forced the butterfly to appear, all crumbled, before its time. It struggled desperately and a few seconds later, died in the palm of my hand.

> *That little body is, I do believe, the greatest weight I*
> *have on my conscience. For I realize today that it is a*
> *mortal sin to violate the great laws of nature. We should*
> *not hurry, we should not be impatient, but we should*
> *confidently obey the eternal rhythm.*[6]

I do believe that one of the most immediate destroyers of new life is too much control, too much organization: We know what is needed; we cannot wait for it to unfold; we want to organize it; we want to take charge. In so doing, we rush the birth, and frequently we abort it.

In Part I ("The Danger of Denial"), I suggested that the denial of passage to the new kills it. I asked whether we are willing to go into labor and to birth new life, or whether we will choke it instead because we resist letting go. An equally serious hazard presents itself when we speed up the process; when we try to control what cannot be controlled, bureaucratize what needs to be allowed to happen without the "formal approval" that risks boxing it in; when we standardize and therefore stifle what requires creative emergence instead. Both when we deny passage as well as when we hurry it, we kill. In either case there is excessive control and paradoxically, as in the case of the butterfly, we can even, in prematurely taking charge of the birthing process, deny "labor" by rushing it.

Recently I heard of a newly appointed "formation" director who left a promising and fruitful position so that she could devote herself full time to the guiding and "forming" of the two "novices" in her charge. The question that came to me was whether the "novices" had been consulted about their need for such extraordinary generosity. A less kind thought came from a sense of "overkill" that frustrated me, and that had me question whether "novices" who require such seemingly excessive care-taking would, in fact, be desirable candidates for the religious life that is emerging. What do we think our newer members need when we put so much energy into their "formation"? Is this much attention really needed; is it in fact welcome?

In many religious congregations, especially of women, the call to religious life seems frequently now to be a second career — something chosen in response to the depth experience of the second journey. Prospective newer members often have already had major relational experiences when they come to us. They have at times been married, raised children. They often are professional persons who have made important decisions in their lives; have an education; have savings, cars, insurances; have traveled, ministered, loved; have a spirituality and know how to pray. Their interest in us is stimulated quite frequently be-cause they already are drawn by the charism that, albeit often unconsciously, made them look at our congregation rather than at another one. More than anything else, they are probably quite aware of what they need, and if they are not, would like a chance to find out for themselves. They would then, it seems to me, be quite willing to express it if we gave them half a chance. Many of them are uncomfortable with the "hothouse" atmosphere that surrounds their entrance requirements and would probably pre-fer it if their directors lived elsewhere and had a full or at least a part-time ministry besides that of introducing them to religious life. This would permit breathing space, give newer members room for a bit of originality in their years of discernment, and allow them to make a few decisions for themselves instead of having every minutia decided for them.

It has been my experience that new members often find it difficult to decline when the needs others perceive them to have are being taken care of "for their own good." They find it trying to respond to the general rules drawn up for all "novices" because the membership at large or the leadership team have decided that these are beneficial for them. Many of them have already had the experiences we prescribe for them and would love to share with us some of the insights with which they come. They often have wisdom from which we all could benefit. Our newer members for the most part are adults accustomed to be part of the decision making that affects their lives. They see our "formation" requirements as unpleasant attempts at infantalization.

During a conversation we had some time ago, a mature woman (the only newer member in her community) mentioned to me how difficult she had found it to communicate to her much younger director that she did not share the latter's need to see her for guidance every week. Many newer members cannot bring themselves to such honesty but experience the same discomfort. They are in a new environment that often feels quite foreign to them. They find it hard enough to get their bearings without having to worry about hurting the feelings of an overprotective and often well-meaning director.

Recently during a weekend workshop I was giving, the "novices" from a rather large community requested some private time with me to process some of the material. I gladly spent the early afternoon with them and their director but found them unusually resistant. During the break at a later session with the whole community, the woman who seemed to have been the most opposed to my comments at the earlier meeting shared with me privately that, in fact, "all of us agree with you, but when one's director is present, one can't always say what really is on one's mind." Something like this is sad and smacks of the regressive behavior that invariably accompanies institutionalization. It is the "grin-and-bear-it attitude" I already discussed in Part I ("On Tying Up the Cat"). Nevertheless, most of us continue to insist that initiation rights and procedures for our newer members follow the hierarchical model that our archaic concept of "formation" of necessity points to. We bureaucratize their welcome, institutionalize their training in the name of tradition, and mistakenly conclude that the dysfunctional behavior often induced by our regimentation is doubtlessly due to a character flaw that requires counseling, therapy, or even dismissal. Is it not strange that so many newer members, who have often functioned successfully in the stressful conditions of our contemporary world, are required to get therapy once they join us? What is wrong with this picture?

It is clear, of course, that the depth encounter with oneself is frequently enhanced by therapy, and that many of us, especially during the second half of our lives, have benefited from having someone trained to help the inner healing process walk with us. The rate at which this seems to be mandated of newer members, often in the very first years of "formation," is nevertheless troubling to me, particularly since it is a requirement frequently imposed upon them for their continued welcome in the congregation. Might it not be that, at least on occasion, dysfunctionality brings out dysfunctionality? I, for one, find it difficult to respond to remarks about the supposed regressive behavior or immaturity of those attracted to religious life today without recalling an elementary dictum from teachers' college: If you want honesty, discipline, kindness, and most of all maturity, model it and, furthermore, expect it. For better or for worse, most persons react in kind. We see ourselves reflected in the eyes of others and tend to live "up" or "down" accordingly.

Why is it that even if we attract newer members — something that happens largely through our ministries — most of them ultimately leave? Could it be that some at least find their maturity, wholesomeness, and health threatened? Could the problem, at least in part, rest with us? In our conversion toward new life, it seems of primary importance for us to explore what in fact we are inviting newer members to. Our hospitality may require above all making our homes welcoming and empowering places not only for them, but also for ourselves. Peace and well-being in our midst would do much to sustain our witness potential as well as help congregational health and transformation.

In *Where Two or Three Are Gathered* I attempted to address some of the maturity concerns that need to be faced for a healthy life together. Might I suggest that the gender-specific issues we reflected on in Part II ("In God's Image" and "A Tale and a Message") also will affect how we transform our living situations? Perhaps the feminine, when it is allowed to express itself, will resist the somewhat regimented model of togetherness that community life has meant, and may even continue to mean, for so many of us. Nor does our newfound idol of "sharing" at prayer and "consensus decision making" necessarily move away from regimentation, especially when it becomes compulsory and exhausts rather than frees people.

If we want to take seriously the much-needed examination of our lifestyle and of the communal living to which we are inviting newer members, we will not be able to escape the painful questions concerning our institutions and the way we live there. How does institutional living foster growth and well-being? Why is it that large numbers of religious resist it now? Does it encourage relationality, a sense of at-homeness? Are these luxuries that we should have learned to do without, and that newer members should be taught to reject, or are they essential for wholesome living? Do we need to continue to see institutional life as part of religious life? If not, what radical decisions do we need to make for our sake as well as for the sake of meaningful hospitality and the sustaining of new life? Can we make these decisions? Where does our creativity lead us?

Organic Incorporation

I find it interesting that when life-giving communities cannot be found for our newer members, we organize one in order to provide the proper environment. We call it the "formation" community. If we are a large congregation, we often gather "novices" from all the provinces or regions across the country, and sometimes even from abroad, in order to provide for them the perfect setting to learn what religious life is all about. In many respects, this saves professional personnel for us and gives new members the opportunity for bonding and experiencing the kind of community life that would otherwise be difficult to find. There is a great deal of good intention here, but where is the reality?

To begin with, what is the point of creating an environment that can only be found with difficulty in the rest of the congregation? *What is it* about the "formation" community that can generally not be found elsewhere, and if it cannot be found, why are we presenting it as normative? Aside from the fact that one might perceive this as somewhat deceptive, one might also wonder whether it is not doomed to failure. If indeed there are no other communities to equal the "formation" house, what are the newer members to do after the one year or so of an experience they will never or rarely have again? Are they to "model" it when they join the less normative communities and, if so, are we not setting them up? Will we be surprised when newer members who have, in fact, liked the experience in the "formation" house, become disillusioned and frustrated once they discover it is not real?

A second question of concern revolves around the kind of welcome we are here envisioning. Does one need trained persons to welcome adults into a community of equals? Is there a bureaucratic element here that is out of place? What is the symbolic message of this for the congregation? Might the rest of us not be tempted to think that if professionals are there to do the job, why is there a need for us to worry or to care? We are all busy people and need the little time we have to re-create ourselves. We can, therefore, presume that since the congregation has appointed someone qualified to the "full-time" job of welcoming these newer members, and since their number is small, we need not bother. Besides that, she or he is well trained for this, and we are not.

The bureaucratization of welcome destroys it. Ultimately, no one gets involved: While the congregation leaves it to the "formation" community, professional directors know that in their position it is inappropriate to "befriend" those for whom they are responsible. They therefore keep their distance. Should the newer members have come from another part of the country, they have left their support systems behind — their family, their friends, and the members of the community they knew and cared for. Aside from the few professed who live in the "formation" community, they have then only the other newer members with whom to relate. These know as little as they do about the congregational workings, may be equally "displaced," and may be experiencing as much stress. Often newer members are few in number. They do not automatically feel the attraction to bond with one another or those made available to them in the "formation" house. They may also realistically not wish to put the energy into something that will of necessity end after one year. All new members will then be sent back to the provinces or regions from which they came and, after that, will have to fend for themselves in a now largely foreign and politely indifferent community. For welcome to be effective it has to be sustained. It is rarely experienced in relational settings that are short lived. It cannot be expressed by proxy, but has to be expressed by the people with whom one "throws in one's lot." Professional "welcome communites" appear for the most part artificial and are ultimately self-defeating.

Thirdly, if a congregation's active members predominantly live in small groups or alone, and if someone is drawn to join such a congregation, would it not be only logical that the small group setting is the reality that ought to be presented? It seems to me that if we truly want membership, we will work out realistic modes of welcome within the context of our lives. To re-create what was is to present a nonexistant ideal and to belie the present situation. Furthermore, until we seriously consider the paradigm into which religious life seems to be evolving and work with it creatively, we render an additional disservice to newer members by holding them to past models and depriving them of new, creative ways of living and feeling included. It may be of value during this time of transition to inquire among those of our members now living singly or in twos how they have worked out their need to be part of the larger community, how they bond, how they have learned to address their relational needs. All this could be helpful in getting a new perspective on welcoming the contemporary woman or man into our midst in different but perhaps more realistic ways.

In *Living the Vision* I reflected on the possibility of "organic" rather than "institutional" or systemic incorporation. I told the story of the rabbi who lived in the woods close to an old and dying monastic community. One day he told the monks the precious secret that "the Messiah was in their midst." In the transformation that this news brought to their vision, not only of themselves but also of one another and of everyone who visited them, new life was born in their midst.[7] It grew gently and in silence. It was a sacred event that, in the truest sense and much to their surprise and wonder, happened upon them rather than being orchestrated by them. But it happened gradually, as transformation is wont to — in "the eternal rhythm of things."

It is my conviction that new life in religious congregations today will happen that way as well, or it will not happen at all. Life is an organic phenomenon that flourishes where it is welcome and where the environment is right. It resists external control, strategies, and artificiality. It cannot be forced and retain its integrity. It does not fit into a preordained schedule. "Organic incorporation means that the women or men interested in our life-style are simply invited to be the women or men *they* are, among the women or men *we* are, with all the risks that growing together implies."[8] Speaking to women about the normal growth process that engages all of us, Pam Finger says it well:

You do not have to be your mother unless she is who
you want to be. You do not have to be your mother's
mother, or your mother's mother's mother, or your
grandmother's mother on your father's side. ... *[Y]ou
are not destined to become the women who came before
you. You are not destined to live their lives.* So if you
inherit something, *inherit their strength, their resilience.*
Because the only person you are destined to become is
the person you decide to be.[9]

Her wisdom pertains to men as well, of course. They also
do not need to be their fathers or their father's father, but have to
find their own originality. Applied to our situation, the message
is clear: Growth into a religious vocation, just as healthy growth
into adulthood, is deeply personal even as it involves a community. The community upon which it depends must be made up
of the real flesh-and-blood individuals of the present moment
with whom one covenants, each also growing into her or his
uniqueness. True discernment is with them but is also individu-
alized. It spans over years. "[T]he 'religious' emerges out of
each new member slowly, and stamps the congregation each
time with originality."[10] The setting for the emergence needs to
be the setting to which the individual belongs, made up of sisters or brothers who support but do not invade the process.

We all know, of course, that the "religious" may also *not*
emerge out of the new member, but this ought not necessarily
mean that the bonds with the congregation have to be severed.
Given new models of membership, the individual and those with
whom she or he is discerning may simply discover that another
form of connectedness is called for. Here, once again, it is

essential that the welcome we offer is into our *lived reality*. I firmly believe that the time for idealized and controlled experiences is over and that no one is served by them. An honest encounter from the start with what is real is a much better guarantee of perseverance in the long run, since it honors the maturity of those interested in religious life and fosters the honesty all of us need in this difficult time of transition. The diversity and change we are experiencing today *is* our reality, and newer members should see it *as such*. They do not need to be presented with the "right" formula since, given what we have discussed so far, that may be difficult if not impossible to identify and may prove to be either nostalgic or deceptive.

The question that faces us today is well stated by Margaret J. Wheatley in her brilliant study, *Leadership and the New Science*: "How do we create structures that move with change, that are flexible and adaptive, even boundaryless, that enable rather than constrain? ... How do we resolve personal needs for freedom and autonomy with organizational needs for prediction and control?"[11] In a world that presences itself as progressively more organic and ever less mechanistic, where "[d]ynamic events, not unchanging substances, are now taken to constitute reality,"[12] relationality and interdependence are rapidly claiming primary consideration. An ancient Sufi saying may help us grasp what this implies for us: "You think because you understand *one* you must understand *two*, because one and one makes two. But you must also understand *and*."[13] The *and* is the key to comprehending the nature of welcome between a congregation *and* the new. It speaks of a unity of mutual implication that reverences a dynamic process of relationship and thus furthers creativity and life.

In Search of the "Why"

W isdom figures through the ages have told us that knowing the "why" usually helps us live through any "how." With respect to the dirth of religious vocations, it seems that, after all is said and done, there nevertheless remains the question, "Why?" As with the old monastic community of the previous reflection, not understanding the reason is known to bring discouragement and frustration, and frequently deenergizes us to the point of actually moving us toward the very demise we dread so much. Often, also, there is much guilt about not having done it right; about having to fix it somehow, so that once again interested persons will join us to live out the charism of our founder. The issues we have already discussed point in the direction of the "why," but focus more on our way of responding to new members when they do come to covenant with us, as well as on allowing for greater inclusion of those already interested. The reason why so few seem to be coming may, however, still demand a more direct reflection. And here our insights do not necessarily have to be negative, for there seem to be numerous reasons why religious life is declining in the West.

I

To begin with, the cultural as well as the economic development in this region of the world needs to be considered: It has had a powerful influence on women in particular and therefore on religious communities of women as well. Most women in the Western hemisphere today can do the work for which religious communities of women were founded — without having to join such a group. The emancipation of women has brought this about, and we can proudly acknowledge that we had something to do with this. Every one of our founders was an emancipator, a liberator. Although few women religious may have realized it at the time, the economic advantages for women — the educational and professional possibilities — may have at least partially influenced their decision, as well as their parents' encouragement, to join a religious congregation where teaching, nursing, social work, or administration were possible for them. This in no way diminishes the authenticity of the call. The desire for ministry, the possibility to serve others and help better their condition, as we discussed already in Part II ("Celibate Love"), has traditionally been a trustworthy criterion for vocational discernment. Today, however, the emancipation of women, which allows them to minister where before only religious organizations could facilitate the ministry of women, has been effected. Likewise the emancipation of the laity in general allows men to minister today in positions formerly only held by priests and sometimes by brothers. We have in many ways enabled this emancipation and, by so doing, have, at least to some extent, ministered ourselves out of a way of life. The sadness about our decreasing numbers holds in it, therefore, also a powerful reason for celebration that many of us have not as yet realized.

II

Along with the preceding consideration goes the recognition also that the reason for our decline may quite possibly be climactic. By this I mean that various religious congregations may have reached the end and purpose of their founding. Their work may have reached fulfillment. The ministerial reasons for which their foremothers or forefathers gathered into community may no longer exist. The need for them to minister in a particular way or at a particlar location may no longer be there. Others may now be able to carry on without them. This, in every respect, is cause for celebration, for it indicates a job well done. It is, nevertheless, painful, and a powerful call to releasement — to let go of long cherished ministries or institutions (with which many of us have identified almost as much as with our own congregations) and to get ready for new challenges.

Margaret Wheatley's meditation on a mountain stream in the American Rockies helped me considerably in this regard. While cooling her feet in the swirling water, she asked herself what it is that streams could teach her about organizations:

> I am attracted to the diversity I see, to these swirling combinations of mud, silt, grass, water, rocks. This stream has an impressive *ability to adapt, to shift the configurations, to let the power balance move, to create new structures.* But driving this adaptability, making it all happen, I think, is the water's need to flow. Water answers to gravity, to downhill, to the call of ocean. *The forms change but the mission remains clear. Structures emerge, but only as temporary solutions that facilitate rather than interfere.* There is none of the rigid reliance

on single forms, on true answers, on past practices. ...
Streams have more than one response to rocks; otherwise, there'd be no Grand Canyon. Or else Grand Can-
yons everywhere. The Colorado realized that there were
ways to get ahead other than by staying broad and ex-
pansive.[14]

Wheatley suggests that, like the mountain stream, organizations need faith — "faith that they can accomplish their purposes in various ways and that they do best when they focus on
direction and vision, letting transient forms emerge and disap-
pear." Streams, she suggests, have "sparkling confidence."
"[T]hey know that their intense yearning for ocean will be ful-
filled, that nature creates not only the call, but the answer."[15]
Streams model releasement.

It seems to me that the separate reflection on our mission
and the vision it inspires — not ignoring, but also not necessarily connecting it with traditional congregational ministries —
would do much to help us toward this elusive virtue. It might
enable our accepting new challenges and letting go of what no
longer needs us. This reflection might be in small groups, where
individuals can tell of their dreams, their stories, their hopes,
their vision. It might be over a period of time, with the express
purpose of generating energy through encounter. There may be
no measurable data expected from these encounters except the
increase of love and care and excitement. On the other hand, it
could of course happen that some creative expression might take
shape and would, in due time, be shared with the larger congregation. The purpose, however, is simply to generate life, to share
vision, and to celebrate, rather than to negate the diversification

that has become a reality for us.

Many of us are used to approaching "vision" collectively in terms of an observable and definable future goal that we effect in a causal manner by specific behavior done by all of us now. We ask committees and task forces and even Chapters to define our corporate stance clearly so that all of us can witness to it. We tend to think that commonality here and a certain uniformity in seeing and in action will help us witness to it more successfully. This, many of us think, will bring us newer members as well, since people will once again be able to see what we are about. For some reason, however, we never seem to be able to get very far when we approach "vision" that way. Perhaps we are starting from the wrong end. Perhaps we are missing the mutuality necessary for effective visioning. No one, not even a congregational Chapter, can vision for anyone else. Vision moves from the inside out, not from the outside in. What if we changed the focus, therefore, and saw corporate vision, instead, as a by-product of *each of us expressing the mission in our personal behavior and unique perspective?* What if we came to see each of us as "walking the talk" consistently, wherever we are, whatever we do; each of us as "filling space with the message we are about"; each of us as harmoniously being about mission and energizing one another?

Some interesting discoveries in contemporary science may serve here as metaphors to help us understand this; to take away some of our fear of letting go, as well as our dread of individualism. They may also help to move us toward new forms of consciousness: Benedictine Willigis Jäger, reflecting on morphogenetic fields (invisible fields that determine the forms of organisms) comprising the reality of the universe, assures us that research in both physics and biology points to the realization that "*the part can produce the new whole*." Quoting Rupert Sheldrake, he explains that

> "morphogenetic fields shape and direct the entire animate and inanimate creation. And although the fields are free of matter and energy, they still have an effect on space and time, and can even be changed over space and time. If a member of a biological species acquires a new behavior, its morphogenetic field will be altered. *If it retains its new behavior long enough, the morphic resonance will set up a reciprocal effect among all the members of the whole species.* The morphogenetic fields are the actual cause of the order, regularity, and constancy of the universe — but *they can also admit wholly new modes and forms of behavior.*" Thus we are not primarily physiological and biological creatures, but beings with a fundamentally spiritual structure.[16]

Experiments show that morphic resonance can be worldwide, even cosmic. The implications for us are astounding! It seems that the effect each one of us has on the whole can be quite staggering and indeed transforming. What if we thought in terms of compassion, mercy, gentleness of heart? What if each one of us would see herself or himself as effecting congregational transformation, as well as the Christification of the cosmos, in the embracing of the mission? As Jäger would have us consider:

As a result of the worldwide influence that these fields have, it seems reasonable to assume that even our ... contemplation has a strong influence on these metastructures. In other words, *we can change humanity, society, and the world by our ... changing ourselves.* Anyone who enters upon one of the esoteric paths of the great religions is performing the actual work of changing consciousness in our world.

Mystics have always been clear on this point. The silent prayer of men and women who betake themselves into the presence of God is far stronger and far more powerful than many words. Such persons are, as it were, connecting themselves to God's field of force and becoming conductors of energy to others. We have to learn to become open to this divine source of energy, to which every one of us is linked.[17]

Our reflections on agapic love and our celibate response (Part II, "Celibate Love") come to mind once again. Divine love in each of us radiates outward. God takes shape in us and through us in the world. Our congregational commitment rests on our personal fidelity. The whole is only as strong as each part.

If indeed the love of God impels all of us, and faith in this fact is what holds us together, then working within a common vision, a realistic field of possibilities already experienced deep within each one of us and shared precisely because of that, gives energy to what we are about, no matter with what specific ministry we are involved. It allows for our diversity, even as it fosters unity and solidarity among us and strengthens our witness potential. The "ocean" that calls us will be what matters to us. It will be already present in our being. How we move toward it and in it will be left to our originality, our gifts, our talents, our energy. And here our numbers will be less important than the manner of our presence.

III

Perhaps the ocean metaphor we have been considering will provide us with still a third reason for our diminishment. We might identify it quite simply as a "focus shift" in our congregational life, and suggest that many of us may in fact be no longer about what we *claim* to be about, that in some respects we no longer feel the pull of the ocean. Now, "what we lose when we fail to create consistent messages, when we fail to 'walk the talk,' is not just personal integrity. We lose the *partnership of a field-rich space* that can help bring form and order to the [congregation]."[18] It seems that such a loss inevitably brings with it confusion and loss of energy. One example of this may be that we may not really any longer be serving the poor in greatest need, or truly be doing "with less until everyone has enough." Our institutions may no longer witness to charity, or mercy, or the goodness of God, but may instead be corporations — big businesses — and *this* may be the reason for our decline and call to conversion. On the other hand, instead of being the reason for it, our low witness potential may also, at least partially, be the result of our decline. We may no longer have the energy or the personnel to do the work or even supervise it. We may also not have arrived yet at other creative ways to be about the mission. And here only clear-headed honesty, as well as profound humility, can help us.

For a second example to illustrate our focus shift, we may

wish to reflect once again on our community situations. Could it be that, for whatever reason, we are no longer able to foster the communities necessary for adult growth and maturation, or even for the flourishing of new life? Has our community life atrophied, or is what we were used to as community life — the behavior patterns and ways of approaching togetherness — no longer viable today? Is our community life in need of radical rethinking or regrounding?

Many of the issues related to a possible focus shift may also be connected with our overall aging and our general fatigue. It takes energy to welcome younger people (if these, in fact, are still attracted to us), to bridge a very clear generation gap. There arises, therefore, as we have discussed already, the very real temptation to leave the job to the one or two well-trained directors whose "ministry" it is. As a result, the bridging of generations or cultures in our local communities never happens and new members rarely, if ever, really feel welcome. Nor do they experience a sense of belonging. They feel condescension instead, for often decisions are made for them in terms of how they are viewed and interpreted by us, without serious regard for their insights or opinions. Their much-needed input regarding new models of interacting is rarely accepted by us, therefore, if indeed it is acknowledged at all.

Much to my joy, an exception here came to my attention just as I was in the process of writing this chapter. A new member with whom I had worked during a retreat some months ago wrote to me to tell me that she was making her final commitment shortly, and that she had been asked to join her congregation's "formation" team. Her first successful undertaking, she told me, had been to remove the entire "evaluation" component in the policy manual for "formation" and to replace it with one simple line about "discernment in process." It was her way of restoring dignity and of expressing the expectation of maturity to newer members; to move toward reciprocity between the newer members and the community. This kind of courage gives me hope.

For vibrancy and life, for true conversion, we need to allow the *new* scope for expression. We need to recognize the root of unhappiness in our own communities and place it squarely at the feet of our own inability and, sometimes, perhaps, our unwillingness to face and to accept the numerous challenges that diversity — in age, in culture, in race, in language, in education, and even in theology and spirituality — presents to us. "There are no recipes or formulae, no checklists or advice that describe 'reality,'" and will therefore solve our dilemma. "There is only what we create through our engagement with others and with events."[19] Margaret Wheatley's Rocky Mountain stream has much to teach us: Adaptation, diversity, letting the power balance move, creating new structures are all means toward realizing the vision. They are not ends in themselves. They do not need to be feared. They open up, rather, to exciting possibilities — to life.

Creativity and Courage

I sit in a room without windows, participating in a ritual etched into twentieth-century tribal memory. I have been here thousands of times before, literally. I am in a meeting, trying to solve a problem. Using whatever analytic tool somebody has just read about or been taught at their most recent training experience, we are trying to come to grips with a difficult situation. ... The topic doesn't matter. What matters is how familiar and terrible our process is for coming to terms with the complaint.

The room is adrift in flip chart paper — clouds of lists, issues, schedules, plans, accountabilities — crudely taped to the wall. They crack and rustle, fall loose, and, finally, are pulled off the walls, tightly rolled, and transported to some innocent secretary, who will litter the floor around her desk so that, peering down from her keyboard, she can transcribe them to tidy sheets, which she will mail to us. They will appear on our desks days or weeks later, faint specters of commitments and plans, devoid of even the little energy and clarity that sent the original clouds — poof — up onto the wall. They will drift into our day planners and onto individual "to do" lists, lists already fogged with confusion and inertia. *Whether they get "done" or not, they will not solve the problem.*

I am weary of the lists we make, the time projections we spin out, the breaking apart and putting back together of problems. *It does not work.* The lists and charts we make *do not capture experience. They only tell of our desire to control a reality* that is slippery and evasive and perplexing beyond comprehension. Like bewildered shamans, we perform rituals passed down to us, hoping they will perform miracles. No new wisdom teacher has appeared to show us how to fit more comfortably into the universe. Our world grows more disturbing and mysterious, our failures to predict and control leer back at us from many places, yet to what else can we turn? If the world is not linear, then our approaches cannot work. But then, where are we?[20]

There is a ring of familiarity in this account from *Leadership and the New Science.* Although Wheatley here speaks to corporations in general, most of us know the setting all too well and are familiar with the inertia, the flip charts, the watered-down summaries of small group sharings that once may have had food for thought but now are simply more of the same. We are tired not only after, but often, also, *before* congregational meetings. "What is the point?" many of us ask. We are happy to see one another, and frequently this is the main reason why we keep coming, but the meetings drag on. Organizers, ever with the best intentions, assure us that something new will happen this time, that issues *will* be addressed and structures *have to* be changed.

Sometimes, to endure the tedium, we call our gatherings by new names: We suggest that they are "feminine," or "holistic," or "ecological," and we do the peripheral things. We cut down on the donuts and put out fruit. We invite everyone to bring her or his own mug. Our prayer services use inclusive language, and we insist on consensus for our discussions. But the flip charts remain and so do the summaries. The process is structured and thoroughly defined ahead of time, and we all "honor" it regardless of whether it fits. After all, we need control over something! Somehow we feel compelled to organize and structure even our chaos and the breakdown of meaning or purpose, in spite of the fact that we feel the rug being pulled from under our feet. And so we keep at it. We call the group together over and over. We keep working at organizational reorganization — "government plans," we call them. And we ask an ever greater number of our active sisters to work internally in order to get it all done. And all the while we ignore the fact that "no problem can be solved from the same consciousness that created it."[21]

Not long ago at a regional Chapter meeting I found myself in a highly stimulating smaller discussion group. Much went on during our meeting that had little to do with what had been planned for us, but we all seemed to feel surprisingly energized. We shared deeply with one another about our ministries, about struggles as well as joys we had experienced, about congregational experiences. We *met* each other and felt a common bond. All of us knew that we wanted more of this kind of encounter and that we wanted others to experience it as well. We clearly sensed that exchange such as we were experiencing would be fruitful for all of us even if its outcome could not be predicted or summarized. And yet some of us surmised also that, if exchanges were organized for us and promoted as congregational "sharing sessions" without some eventual goal, many of us might consider ourselves too busy to come.

There is a great need for spontaneity among us even as we keep hankering after order. Our resistance to determinism and control, therefore, seems often unrecognized and frequently manifests itself not through belligerence or planned opposition, but through fatigue and a loss of energy. It seems that our bodies, perhaps more so than our intellects, crave creativity and almost instinctively know that too much organization and need for the definite, for finality and closure, thwarts life. Ian Barbour, writing about the laws of physics, describes our situation with uncanny accuracy: "An ordered system," he points out, has "lower probability, and higher information content. ... In closed systems, *order* and *information* are dissipated over time. On a cosmic scale this is referred to as the 'running down' of the universe."[22]

Clearly, order and, therefore, information are not what is lacking in our gatherings. Information abounds. Unfortunately, however, we often demand it to the point of minutia, so that quantity does not match quality. Thus, life and energy — that which invites newness — does not seem to be generated at our meetings. Might we say that, from a symbolic perspective, our universe is running down? The difficulty we experience with diversity and with the accepting of new forms of membership, furthermore, seems to make ours a rather closed system. Barbour informs us that normally living systems, although they have a high degree of order and information, nevertheless evolve and develop. This is "because *they are open rather than closed.*"[23] Is there a lesson in this for us? Finally, although we may find it hard to believe, the discovery of contemporary science shows that randomness and disorder allow for creativity. A "disordered system has high probability (because there are many arrangements of the constituents by which it can be achieved) and low information content (since it appears random)."[24] Randomness and seeming chaos at one level, however, "[lead] to dynamic patterns at another level." Often "there are many possible outcomes, and no unique prediction can be made. Multiple divergent solutions arise from these nonlinear instabilities. ... [T]here seems to be a complex interplay of law and chance."[25] Openness, then — the acceptance of diversity and the letting go of too much control and predictability — might stand us in good stead and may restore much-needed energy and life to our "system."

Sadly enough, the symbolic message contained in these discoveries from contemporary physics escapes many of us. We cannot as yet see with the eyes of modern science and hold on, instead, to our seventeenth-century categories of linear and rational thought; of graphs, and charts, and maps; of clear and distinct ideas; of analysis — a "reduction into parts and the proliferation of separation."[26] We want to understand things, even ourselves, that way. (Our concern about membership — who is in, who is out — is a clear case in point.) We want to plan ahead and have a precise delineation of power. The Cartesian and Newtonian world view has been our home base for three hundred years. We see through it, think with its categories, interact on its terms. Many of us cannot even comprehend that there may be a different way of seeing and of doing. Yet the difficult issues facing us and their seeming persistence indicate that a change is necessary.

In *Where Two or Three Are Gathered*, I suggested that the dilemma we are experiencing is opening up a profound opportunity for transformation, for conversion toward a new way of approaching not only ourselves but all of reality. This new way is still partly unknown, though it seems to point away from functionality toward relational ways of interacting. Because it is still unfolding, it requires patience as well as vigilance and calls us "to abide in the waiting."[27] Part One of this book speaks to this waiting as well ("A Time for Courageous Waiting"), and attempts to offer questions to help us move into the core issues concerning our life together. It is clear that waiting ought not to be equated with idleness. The emphasis here is on openness, on a resistance to finality, on the ability to look wherever the possibility for new insight reveals itself. This is the time for "think-tanks," for interdisciplinary and intercongregational studies and reflections, for open-endedness and dialogue. This is the time for daring, for creativity.

Within this context, it seems that the discoveries and the symbology of modern physics provide us with surprisingly new ways of seeing. Already a number of studies in various fields, including transpersonal psychology and spirituality, are using its insights. Unfortunately, many of us have been relatively unaware of the impact science has had on our way of seeing. After all, until fairly recently, religion and science have not been on friendly terms. They have, in fact, been rather antagonistic. The all-pervasive impact of Newtonian categories, therefore, remained unconscious for us, though it was effective nonetheless. Our attachment to stability, along with our need for clarity, for closure and certainty, for the measurable and calculable, are not necessarily "merely human," therefore; they are expressions, in fact, of a particular way of seeing that has dominated history for centuries and that has enveloped us almost in spite of ourselves. If they fail us today, it is not necessarily the total collapse of truth as such, but merely of one approach to it. Other modes of seeing may be ready to reveal themselves to us and to invite our creativity out of its demise. It is time for us to "seize the day."

Fritjof Capra identifies the quantum world as one of "dynamic patterns continually changing into one another — the continuous dance of energy."[28] It is a world that thrives on relationality and resists predictability. It is a world that reveals reality as made up, not of material particles as such, but rather of "probability patterns, interconnections in an inseparable cosmic web that *includes the human observer and her [his] consciousness*."[29] The way we look at reality, therefore, ultimately determines it. "The observed patterns of matter are reflections of patterns of mind."[30] Concepts such as the essential relationality of reality, the importance of consciousness in affecting the world and its self-revelation, morphogenetic fields, the dynamic presence of the whole in each part ["Every particle consists of all other particles," not as "separate entities but [as] interrelated energy patterns in an ongoing dynamic process."[31]], though rather complex and beyond the scope of detailed discussion here, have nevertheless profound implications for us, both individually and congregationally. They challenge us beyond cause-and-effect functionality toward holistic and essentially relational consciousness. "Even in its infancy stages," Kathleen Durkin points out, the new science reveals an emerging paradigm of the universe dynamically oriented toward wholeness, toward understanding the system as system in which *relationships are the critical key*, that signals participation in the creative process, and *where life happens in the engagement rather than from outside controls*.[32]

Today we know that order and change, autonomy and control, need not necessarily be understood as opposites. We live, rather, in a world of constant change and ongoing creation that reveals to us ever new ways of bringing about order and structure.[33] Here is where our congregational energy should focus.

It takes courage and creativity for religious institutions consciously to embrace the insights that emerge out of a twentieth-century perspective of reality; to let go of the old, by which many of our holiest customs were interpreted (see Part I, "The Need for 'Core' Involvement"), and to risk the new. In many respects it means stretching ourselves and dropping our defenses. It means accepting the failure of approaches that have brought us to where we are today. It means taking seriously what social analysts, historians, economists, theologians, and artists, as well as philosophers and scientists, are calling the emerging postmodern era.

In transcending dualism and the "metaphor of the world as a machine," a holistic view of reality abandons "the idea of physics as the basis of all science," though it takes its findings seriously and learns from them. It accepts the fact that "different but *mutually consistent* concepts may be used to describe different aspects and levels of reality, without the need to reduce the phenomena of any level to those of another."[34] This interdisciplinary approach allows us to learn and benefit from one another; to use analogy and metaphor, and to open ourselves to an ever deeper and wider mutuality in the fullness of our humanity. It furthermore abolishes distinctions between secular and sacred sciences and furthers the common search for understanding and depth. In this way it fosters the sisterhood and brotherhood of humankind and the interdependence of all of creation.

What if our congregational approaches and our self-studies and surveys were to move away from the accumulation of facts and data — what Wheatley calls "the 'things' of knowledge"— to focus instead on "relationships as the basis of all definitions"?[35] What if we would surrender our need for control and predictability and begin to see and treat reality, including ourselves, as "bundles of potentiality" instead? Would not our life together become exciting again? "None of us exists independent of our relationships with others. Different settings and people evoke some qualities from us and leave others dormant. In each of these relationships we are different, new in some way."[36] The creative potential in such a shift in perspective is enormous and, although we are using quantum physics as our primary metaphor here, our resultant behavior would prove to be remarkably personalist. The uniqueness of each of us — our gifts, our interests, our field of influence — would no longer be seen as threatening. Nor would diversity in living arrangements or ministry necessarily be viewed as individualism. When basic atomism gives way to essential relationality, the juxtaposition of the individual and the community dissipates. "Who is more important, the system or its members?" becomes a non-question. Neither is "above" the other, because one exists only in terms of the other. "What is critical is the *relationship* created between the person and the setting. That relationship will always be different, will *always evoke different potentialities.* It all depends on the players and the moment."[37] Nothing can be determined. Creativity here lies in the element of surprise, in the new. That "formation" programs and evaluation criteria will need major reconsideration, given such a shift in consciousness, seems beyond doubt. Persons are not isolated entities meant to fit into predesigned slots. Each of us is a dynamic openness, a potential of response-ability. The "players and the moment" create numerous variables that no formula can hold in check or predict.

What the world of philosophy has struggled with throughout the ages in terms of "unity in diversity," the subatomic world identifies for us today as the "principle of complementarity," as well as the "uncertainty principle." When we seek out matter as localized in space, when we measure position, it presents itself differently to us than when we study it as momentum. In the first case it appears as particle; in the second case as wave. Matter, however, is both. Its self-revelation depends on us. Reality, indeed, "gives us what we are looking for." Unfortunately, however, we can never see it both ways simultaneously, and thus certainty eludes us.[38] It seems important, then, not to come down on either side and absolutize it, since stressing one at the expense of the other distorts the picture. For centuries, of course, we have done precisely that. Uncertainty has never been popular — not in science, not in religion, not in religious congregations. In all areas of our life, therefore, we are faced today with the need for releasement.

This quantum metaphor symbolizes for us much about our

response both to the world and to each other. The principle of complementarity teaches us that what we say about others speaks also of us. Truth is a relationship between the observer and the observed. Our readiness to evaluate others, especially our newer members, may therefore give us pause for thought. Our evaluations and the forms we draw up for them tell us more about ourselves than we might care to know. The uncertainty principle should have us realize that the absolutization of any truth violates the process. Any final view of holiness; of the sacred as opposed to the secular; of what religious life has to be; of what exactly is to be understood by poverty, by obedience; of what activity clearly identifies the congregation's charism distorts the picture and destroys any possibility of a viable lifestyle based on such criteria. Unlearning here is essential for us, and suspicion of any formula or program for congregational or individual development based on these criteria is warranted.

The essential relationality between us and our environment, if accepted and acknowledged by us, will clearly affect congregational self-studies, objectives, and renewals — what we will wish to discuss, and where we will want to put our energies. As organizational theorist Karl Weick points out: "The environment that the organization worries about is put there by the organization."[39] We are responsible for our surroundings, not in the absolute sense of creator, but rather by evoking or suppressing its potential.[40] Our emphasis, therefore, needs to shift from non-existent objective data, from truths or falsehoods in themselves — things that stand, independent of us, for our consideration — to a focus on practicality, "on issues of effectiveness, on questions of what happened, and what actions might have served us better. We could stop arguing about truth and get on with figuring what works best,"[41] what speaks to the issue and is relevant for the moment.

That much of what we discussed in Part I concerning "tradition" and the "regrounding of our values" applies here should be clear. Regrounding will often demand heart-wrenching wrestling at the very core of our being. Truth, for us, was never merely an objective category, but a sacred category as well — identified with Being and ultimately with God. It was out there, to be attained. One could have it or not have it. One had to strive for it. To see it now as a relationship that involves the one who quests after it is difficult to fathom, let alone condone. The Sufi tale we reflected on at the end of Part I ("The God Who Appears at Dawn") may, therefore, once gain need to direct us to what God really wants of us above and beyond sacred names and categories: Our God wants burning.

Weick suggests that our new approach needs to emphasize the primacy of action:

> Acting should precede planning ... because it is only through action and implementation that we create the environment. Until we put the environment in place, how can we formulate our thought and plans? In strategic planning, we act as though we are responding to a demand from the environment; but, in fact ... we *create* the environment through our own strong intentions. Strategies should be just in time ... , supported by more investment in general knowledge, a large skill repertoire, the ability to do a quick study, trust in intuitions.[42]

That such an approach would ask for a thorough rethinking of governance and decision-making traditions seems obvious. We will have to come to rely much more strongly on the expertise in the group — work, as I have mentioned already, with task forces and think tanks called together for specific purposes. Individuals will need to be ready for such temporary service to the congregation and will need to be given the power for experimentation and implementation. Congregations may need to inventory the educational experience and talents of their members and call on them frequently. Strategic planning has for too long based itself on the presumption of objective reality. Wheatley assures us, however, that this hard-to-grasp world makes definitions difficult precisely because they are misplaced. "The world is not a thing. It's a complex, never-ending, always-changing tapestry."[43] It is an adventure in which *we* are involved, to which *we* belong. And so:

> We will need to stop describing tasks and instead facilitate *process*. We will need to become savvy about how to build relationships, how to nurture growing, evolving things. All of us will need better skills in listening, communicating, and facilitating groups, because these are the talents that build strong relationships. It is well known that the era of the rugged individual has been replaced by the era of the team player. But this is only the beginning. The quantum world has demolished the concept of the unconnected individual. More and more relationships are in store for us, out there in the vast web of universal connections.[44]

I am reminded once again of the numerous small-group meetings that we have organized for ourselves during our congregational assemblies for the sake, clearly, of furthering relationships. But, as I already pointed out, the creativity evoked there invariably lands on walls in large gathering places, where it is reported on and loses its spark. What if we could let these meetings truly "generate," let them *be* for the sake of the new? What if we as members knew that our creativity at these meetings were truly taken seriously? What if we could somehow take responsibility for this creativity beyond the tedium of reporting? What if the energy generated there could break out into action *before* it would have to be explained, defined, and invariably tucked away onto a list of meaningless and powerless ideas for later consideration? "Acting should precede planning," Weick tells us. This is how the environment is created. Consider the university campus where paths were paved only after students had identified them in walking from building to building. What paths into our tomorrow will we allow ourselves to create that way?

Categories of power identified through tasks, functions, and hierarchical offices no longer hold creative vitality for us. Power is energy and points to "the capacity generated by relationships." Confining it to functions relegates it to what in *Where Two or Three Are Gathered* I have referred to as the very level of consciousness whose demise is responsible for the very crisis in which we find ourselves today.[45] Beatrice Bruteau's "participatory" consciousness is described there as pointing to a sharing of life energy; to a "single large life" that is "a community of whole unique selves who freely form and constitute this large unifying life by the intercommunication of their creative love

energies."[46] Organizational theory speaks of "participative management" and "self-managed teams." Big industry is envisioning and implementing these concepts already. There one hears
of a "boundaryless company" as the successful, relation oriented,
inclusive company of today: "It is this elimination of boundaries between businesses and the transferring of ideas from one
place in the Company to another that is at the heart of what we
call 'integrated diversity.'"[47] Trust in the creative potential of
everyone fosters life energy and new vision. This potential needs
to be nurtured and allowed expression. It does not flourish with
extraneous control and excessive supervision.

> What gives power its charge, positive or negative, is the
> quality of relationships. Those who relate through co-
> ercion, or from a disregard for the other person, create
> negative energy. Those who are open to others and who
> see others in their fullness create positive energy. *Love
> in organizations, then, is the most potent source of power
> we have available.*[48]

And love in religious communities is too. What is religious
life today if it does not witness to this?

Questions for Focus, Reflection, and Discussion

1. Does the vision expressed in transformative element 8, as quoted in "Situating Ourselves," disturb you, or does it energize you? How do you see your congregation realistically moving toward it?

2. Is it true that "congregational documents have a quiet way of slipping into the bottom of drawers or hiding on top shelves, where they gather dust along with indifference"? Is this shocking, sad? If it is true, why is it so?

3. How is it with inclusivity in your community? Is it bringing new energy into your congregation? Whom do you include? Is there anyone whom you exclude — in theory? In practice?

4. Are there in your congregation issues that are somehow inconsistent with what we profess, issues that require honest discussion? Is membership one of these? How seriously would you take a discussion on non-vowed membership or on associate membership with vows appropriate to the life choice, but consistent with the charism? (See "What's Wrong with This Picture?")

5. Is Patricia Wittberg's associational model of membership the predominant model among the active members in your congregation? If not, does it nevertheless have a strong representation? What is your reaction to this? Has your congregation addressed this phenomenon creatively or de-

fensively? What does this choice by so many religious teach us about ourselves?

6. How comfortable are you in "dreaming dreams" about broadening the membership and mission base of the congregation? What are some of your ideas? What is your reaction to some of the ideas suggested in this book? Ultimately, should any model of membership be seen as superior to any other?

7. Does the "formation program" in your congregation reflect the needs of the newer members? Have you ever asked them about it in an environment conducive to honesty? Do newer members have something to teach us, to share with us? Should we draw up general programs for them, or ought they be part of the decisions we make regarding their introduction to religious life? What responsibility do you take to include your newer members in your experiences?

8. What living arrangements do you require of your newer members? Are they reflective of the congregation as a whole? If not, why not?

9. What are your reactions to the invitation to make our homes welcoming and empowering places not only for our newer members but also for ourselves? What might that look like?

10. What are your thoughts on "organic incorporation," on the bureaucratization of welcome as discussed under "Organic Development"?

11. In "In Search of the 'Why,'" several reasons for our decline were discussed. Which ones speak most realistically to you?

12. What is your response to the invitation to small group visioning over a prolonged period of time, and a congregational vision that emerges in the members and is not planned for them? Do you believe that the "effect each one of us has on the whole can be quite staggering and indeed transforming"?

13. What are the lessons of contemporary science concerning the essential relationality of reality? What can they teach us about ourselves and our need for transformation?

14. Do you agree that order and information are not lacking in our congregational meetings, but that openness is required to make ours a viable system? Do creativity and risk, as well as their frequent lack of closure, threaten us? Is this the reason for our decline?

15. How helpful could the principle of complementarity be for our attitude toward communal evaluations and the assessment of our newer members?

16. "We are responsible for our surroundings, not in the absolute sense of creator, but rather by evoking or suppressing its potential." What does this observation teach us about our life together, about our congregational meetings?

17. "Categories of power identified through tasks, functions, and hierarchical offices no longer hold creative vitality for us. Power is energy and points to 'the capacity generated by relationships.'" What, then, do we need to revitalize our togetherness?

Notes

Part I

1. This summary of the story of Parsifal and the Fisher King is extracted from Robert A. Johnson, *He: Understanding Masculine Psychology* (New York: Harper and Row, 1977), and *The Fisher King and the Handless Maiden* (San Francisco: Harper Collins, 1993). There are numerous versions of the Parsifal myth, with some significant differences. I have extracted what seemed important for the purposes of this reflection.

2. Robert A. Johnson, *The Fisher King and the Handless Maiden* (San Francisco: Harper Collins, 1993), pp.15–51.

3. Johnson, p. 20.

4. Frederick Franck, *Messenger of the Heart* (New York: Crossroad, 1976), p. 53.

5. Johnson, p. 46.

6. A discussion on the meaning of inner crucifixion is found in Sebastian Moore, *The Crucified Jesus Is No Stranger* (London: Darton, Longman & Todd, 1977); see also Barbara Fiand, *Embraced by Compassion* (New York: Crossroad, 1993), chapter 4.

7. For more detail regarding the theological significance of these Jungian categories, see Barbara Fiand, *Embraced by Compassion* (New York: Crossroad, 1993), especially chapter 4.

8. Johnson, p. 3.

9. Ibid.

10. Reprinted with permission of author.

11. Barbara Fiand, "Living the Vision: The Present Moment and Future Prospects for Religious Life," in *Religious Life: The Challenge for Tomorrow,* ed., Cassian Yuhaus, C.P. (New York: Paulist Press, 1994), pp. 35–49.

12. The origin of this story is not certain. I first read it in the keynote address, p. 1, given by Sister Marie Chin, R.S.M. to the Sisters of Mercy of Cincinnati, during their 1993 Chapter.

13. Robert Frost, "Mending Wall"; italics mine.

14. Joan Chittister, "Religious life is still alive, but far from the promised land," in *The National Catholic Reporter* 30/16 (February 18, 1994), p. 18.

15. Philip Sheldrake, *Spirituality and History* (New York: Crossroad, 1992), p. 107.

16. Johnson, pp. 9–11.

17. Elizabeth A. Johnson, "Between the Times: Religious Life and the Postmodern Experience of God," in *Review for Religious* 53/1 (January–February 1994), p. 15; italics mine.

18. Robert A. Johnson, p. 35.

19. Chittister, p. 18.

20. Ibid.

21. Ibid.

22. Barbara Fiand, *Releasement: Spirituality for Ministry* (New York: Crossroad, 1987), pp. 48, 49, 50.

23. Ibid.

24. Patricia Wittberg, S.C., *Creating a Future for Religious Life* (New York: Paulist Press, 1991), chapter 3.

25. Barbara Fiand, *Where Two or Three Are Gathered* (New York: Crossroad, 1992), p. 54.

26. Lao Tsu, *Tao Te Ching,* trans. Gia-Fu Feng and Jane English (New York: Vintage Books, 1972), p. 15.

27. Ibid., p. 38; italics mine.

28. Ibid., p. 11; italics mine.

29. Karl Rahner, *The Practice of Faith* (New York: Crossroad, 1983), p. 63; italics mine.

30. Ibid.

31. For a contemporary meditation on the theology of redemption, see Fiand, *Living the Vision*, pp. 29–32.

32. Uta Ranke-Heinemann, *Eunuchs for the Kingdom of Heaven* (New York: Penguin, 1991), p. 184.

33. For an interesting account regarding the origins of dogma in particular, see Elisabeth Schüssler Fiorenza, *Jesus: Miriam's Child, Sophia's Prophet* (New York: Continuum, 1994), pp. 18–24.

34. William Keepin, "Lifework of David Bohm," in *ReVision: A Journal of Consciousness and Transformation* 16/1 (Summer 1993), 34.

35. Friedrich Wilhelm Nietzsche, "The Gay Science," in *The Portable Nietzsche,* ed. Walter Kaufmann (New York: Viking, 1968), aphorism 125, pp. 95, 96.

36. Ranke-Heinemann, chapter IV.

37. T. S. Eliot, *The Dry Salvages.*

38. Ibid.; italics mine.

39. Dorothee Soelle, *Theology for Skeptics: Reflections on God,* trans. Joyce L. Irwin (Minneapolis: Fortress, 1995), pp. 52, 53; italics and emphasis mine.

40. Ibid.

41. Ibid., p. 55.
42. Martin Heidegger, *Holzwege* (Frankfurt Am Main: Vittorio Klostermann, 1963), pp. 248–295. The above was culled from the essay: *"Wozu Dichter."*
43. Soelle, p. 58.
44. Adapted from a tape recording of Sufi Mystical Poetry, read by Coleman Barks, "I Want the Burning," from *Ecstatic World of Rumi, Hafiz, and Lalla* (Boulder, CO: Sounds True Recordings, 1992), tape number A 197.
45. Nicolas Berdyaev, *The Destiny of Man* (New York: Harper Torchbooks, 1960), pp. 28, 29.
46. Ibid.
47. Chittister, p. 16.
48. Soelle, p. 65.
49. Ibid.
50. Ibid., p. 15.
51. Ibid., p. 72.
52. For a discussion of this term as descriptive of systemic domination, see Elisabeth Schüssler Fiorenza, pp. 12–18.
53. Soelle, p. 70.
54. Chin, pp. 15, 16.
55. Ibid.
56. Soelle, p. 73.

Part II

1. There are a great number of scholarly works on this topic. I will cite only four that I have found particularly helpful: Elizabeth A. Johnson, *She Who Is* (New York: Crossroad, 1993); Jann Aldredge Clanton, *In Whose Image?* (New York: Crossroad, 1991); Mary Grey, *Feminism, Redemp-*

tion and the Christian Tradition, (Mystic, CT: Twenty-Third Publications, 1990); Christin Lore Weber, *Woman Christ*, (San Francisco: Harper & Row, 1987).

2. Soelle, pp. 118, 119.
3. Fiand, *Releasement*, p. 59.
4. Cited by Soelle, p. 90.
5. The story is taken from a synopsis by Marie-Louise von Franz, *The Feminine in Fairytales* (Dallas: Spring Publications, 1972), pp. 70–74.
6. Ibid., pp. 82, 83.
7. Weber, p. 8; italics mine.
8. See note 2.
9. von Franz, p. 83.
10. Ibid., p. 84; italics mine. The term "demonic" as used in the citation refers to psychic energy and has no negative theological or religious connotation. For an in-depth understanding of the demonic as well as of "eros," see Rollo May, *Love and Will* (New York: Dell, 1969), pp. 154–158, 160–163, 169–171, 175–176, 320–321.
11. Ibid.
12. Sandra M. Schneiders, "Contemporary Religious Life: Death or Transformation?" in *Religious Life: The Challenge for Tomorrow*, ed. Cassian Yuhaus, C.P. (New York: Paulist, 1994), pp. 9–34.
13. von Franz, pp. 84, 85.
14. Ibid.
15. Ibid., p. 88.
16. Fiand, *Living the Vision,* p. 7.
17. von Franz, p. 85.
18. Ibid., p. 86.

19. Ibid., p. 87.

20. Ibid., p. 89.

21. Pierre Teilhard de Chardin, cited in Jack Canfield and Mark Victor Hansen, *Chicken Soup for the Soul* (Deerfield Beach, FL: Health Communications, 1993), p. 1; italics mine.

22. See Fiand, *Where Two or Three Are Gathered*, chapters I, II; also my article in Yuhaus, *Religious Life: The Challenge for Tomorrow*, pp.35–49.

23. J. E. Cirlot, *A Dictionary for Symbols* (New York: Philosophical Library, 1962), p. 223.

24. Sebastian Moore, *The Crucified Jesus Is No Stranger* (London: Darton, Longman & Todd, 1977), pp. 27, 28.

25. Fiand, *Embraced by Compassion*, p. 129.

26. Ibid.

27. Thomas C. Fox, *Sexuality and Catholicism* (New York: George Braziller, 1995), pp. 163, 164.

28. Francis B. Rothluebber, *Nobody Owns Me: A Celibate Woman Discovers Her Sexuality* (San Diego: Lura Media, 1994). The book takes the form of a journal written during a period of therapy. The author recounts her discovery of her own sexual energy, her overcoming of guilt, her celebration of this, her movement into deeper self-awareness, and recognition of inner strength.

29. Elisabeth Moltmann-Wendel, *I Am My Body: A Theology of Embodiment* (New York: Continuum, 1995), p. 104.

30. Ibid.

31. Sandra M. Schneiders, I.H.M., *New Wineskins, Re-imagining Religious Life Today* (New York: Paulist Press, 1986), p. 114.

32. Fox, p. 181.

33. Thomas Aquinas, *Summa Theologicae,* II/II q 152a. 5 ad 2, cited in Heinemann, p.184.

34. Sheldrake, pp. 60, 61.

35. Schneiders, pp. 114, 115.

36. Ibid., p. 117.

37. Ibid.

38. Ibid., p. 115.

39. John Ferguson, *An Illustrated Encyclopedia of Mysticism and the Mystery Religions* (London: Thames and Hudson, 1976), p. 33.

40. Ibid., p. 174. I have chosen not to make use of gender inclusive pronouns in this citation, in order to accentuate the difficulty and confusion we are discussing.

41. Schneiders, p. 116.

42. Fiand, *Living the Vision*, pp. 89, 90.

43. *Constitutions and Directory,* Sisters of Notre Dame de Namur, p. 25.

44. Gerald G. May, M.D., *Will and Spirit: A Contemplative Psychology* (San Francisco: Harper & Row, 1982), chapter 7.

45. David Richo, *The Marriage of Heaven and Earth: A New Look at Christian Spirituality* (Kansas City, MO: Credence Cassettes), tape 3.

46. May, p. 174.

47. Ibid., pp. 175, 176; italics mine.

48. Viktor E. Frankl, *Psychotherapy and Existentialism* (New York: Washington Square Press, 1967), p. 145.

49. Ibid., p. 147.

50. May, p. 183.

51. Ibid., p. 184.

52. Ibid.
53. Ibid., p. 186.
54. Ibid., p. 185.
55. Ibid., p. 186.
56. Ibid., p. 187.
57. Rudolf Otto, *The Idea of the Holy* (London: Oxford University Press, 1970), p. 23.
58. Ibid., p. 24.
59. See in particular the "transformative elements," in a document entitled *Future of Religious Life*, drafted by the Leadership Conference of Woman Religious and the Conference of Major Superiors of Men in their joined assembly of 1989.
60. Joseph Cardinal Ratzinger, Prefect, Congregation for the Doctrine of the Faith, "Letter to the Bishops of the Catholic Church on the Pastoral Care of Homosexual Persons," Articles 3 and 7.
61. Among numerous books, I recommend Jeannine Grammick and Pat Furey, eds., *The Vatican and Homosexuality, Reactions to the "Letter to the Bishops of the Catholic Church on the Pastoral Care of Homosexual Persons"* (New York: Crossroad, 1988), Robert Nugent: *A Challenge to Love, Gay and Lesbian Catholics in the Church* (New York: Crossroad, 1983).
62. James R. Zullo and James D. Whitehead, "The Christian Body and Homosexual Maturing," in Nugent, op. cit., p. 21.
63. Ibid., p. 25.
64. Ibid.
65. Robert Nugent, "Sexual Orientation in Vatican Thinking,"

in *The Vatican and Homosexuality,* eds. Jeannine Grammick and Pat Furey (New York: Crossroad, 1988), p. 51.

66. Richard Sipe, "Sex and Celibacy," *The Tablet* 246/7914 (May 9, 1992): 576.

67. Ibid.; italics mine.

68. Ibid.

69. Alice Miller, *Prisoners of Childhood* (New York: Basic Books, 1981), p. 15.

70. Fiand, *Living the Vision*; p. 96.

71. May, p. 190; italics mine.

72. William Johnston, *Christian Zen* (New York: Harper Colophon, 1971), p. 94.

73. Ibid.

74. May, p. 173; italics mine.

75. Ibid., p. 128.

76. Erich Fromm, *The Heart of Man* (New York: Harper Colophon, 1964), p. 67.

77. Ibid., p. 69.

78. Ibid., p. 68.

79. May, p. 130.

80. Ibid.

81. Ibid.

82. Ibid.

83. Fiand, *Living the Vision,* p. 64.

84. Ibid., pp. 62, 63.

85. May, pp. 130, 131.

86. St. John of the Cross, *The Living Flame of Love.*

87. Sue Woodruff, *Meditations with Mechtild of Magdeburg* (Santa Fe: Bear & Co., 1982), p. 93.

88. All scientific citations taken from Aniela Jaffé, *The Myth*

of Meaning (New York: Penguin, 1975), pp. 31–35.

89. William Keepin, "River of Truth," *ReVision* 16/1 (Summer 1993): 42.
90. May, p. 131; italics mine.
91. Ibid.
92. Willigis Jäger, *Search for the Meaning of Life* (Liguori, MO: Triumph, 1995), p. 13.
93. Henri J. M. Nouwen, *Clowning in Rome* (Garden City, NY: Image, 1979), p. 37.
94. Ibid., p. 52; italics mine.
95. Karl Rahner, *Theological Investigations, Vol. I,* as cited in *A Rahner Reader,* ed. Gerald A. McCool (New York: Crossroad, 1984), pp. 186, 187.

Part III

1. Joan Chittister, *The Heart of Religious Vocation* (Kansas City, MO: Credence Cassettes, 1995).
2. Allan H. Sager, *Gospel-Centered Spirituality: An Introduction to Our Spiritual Journey* (Minneapolis: Augsburg, 1990), p. 46.
3. Wittberg, p. 71.
4. Ibid., pp. 11, 12. The phrase "intentional community" has of late come to imply a choice of living partners and a common goal for the particular group, chosen by them and drawing them together often from diverse ministries and sometimes even from diverse congregations. Wittberg uses the term technically, referring to traditional community life throughout most of our congregations' histories. She ends her description as follows: "In its most traditional form, an intentional community is also a total

institution, which means that the members live, work and recreate together, having very little contact with persons or ideas from the 'outside world.'"

5. Elisabeth Schüssler Fiorenza, *In Memory of Her* (New York: Crossroad, 1984), pp. 130 and 135.

6. Nikos Kazantzakis, *Zorba the Greek* (New York: Ballantine, 1952), pp. 138, 139.

7. Fiand, *Living the Vision*, pp. 140–143.

8. Ibid., p. 153.

9. Jack Canfield and Mark Victor Hansen, eds, *A 2nd Helping of Chicken Soup for the Soul* (Deerfield Beach, FL: Health Communications, 1995), p. 29; italics mine.

10. Fiand, *Living the Vision*, p. 155.

11. Margaret J. Wheatley, *Leadership and the New Science* (San Francisco: Berrett-Koehle, 1994), p. 8.

12. Ian Barbour, *Religion in an Age of Science* (San Francisco: Harper Collins, 1990), p. 110.

13. Donella Meadows, "Whole Earth Models and Systems;" *Co-Evolution Quarterly* (Summer 1982), p. 23, cited by Wheatley, p. 9.

14. Wheatley, pp. 15, 16; italics mine.

15. Ibid., p. 16.

16. Jäger, p. 26; italics mine.

17. Ibid., p. 27; italics mine.

18. Wheatley, p. 57; italics mine.

19. Ibid., p. 7.

20. Ibid., pp. 25, 26; italics mine.

21. Einstein, cited in Ibid., p. 5.

22. Barbour, pp. 112, 113.

23. Ibid., p. 113; italics mine.

24. Ibid., p. 112.

25. Ibid., p. 113.

26. Wheatley, p. 27.

27. Fiand, *Where Two or Three Are Gathered*, p. 54. The entire book is an exploration of the process of conversion toward a deeper level of consciousness that is beckoning our civilization in general and religious life in particular. See also "Living the Vision: The Present Moment and Future Prospects for Religious Life," in Yuhaus, *Religious Life: The Challenge for Tomorrow*, pp. 35–49.

28. Fritjof Capra, *The Turning Point, Science, Society, and the Rising Culture* (New York: Simon and Schuster, 1982), p. 91.

29. Ibid., pp. 91, 92; italics mine.

30. Ibid., p. 93.

31. Ibid., p. 94.

32. Kathleen Durkin, S.S.J., "A Vicar's View of U.S. Consecrated Life Now and Into The Future," *Sisters Today* 68/1 (January 1996), p. 22; italics mine.

33. Wheatley, p. 2.

34. Capra, p. 97; italics mine.

35. Wheatley, p. 34.

36. Ibid.

37. Ibid.; italics mine.

38. Ibid., p. 35.

39. Karl Weick, *The Social Psychology of Organization* (New York: Random House, 1979), cited in Ibid., p. 37.

40. Ibid., p. 36.

41. Ibid., p. 37.

42. Ibid.

43. Ibid., p. 38.
44. Ibid.
45. Fiand, *Where Two or Three Are Gathered,* pp. 24–29. See also "Living the Vision: The Present Moment and Future Prospects for Religious Life," in Yuhaus, pp. 35–49.
46. Ibid., pp. 75, 76.
47. General Electric letter: "To Our Shareowners," February 15, 1991, p. 2.
48. Wheatley, p. 39; italics mine.